W0082247

~*What was Taken from Me*~

The Rise and Fall of The Lion Series

Tena Duncan

This is a work of fiction. The characters and events in this book are the works of the imagination of the author. Any similarity to a real person, living or dead, is coincidental and not intended by the author.

I dedicate this book to my loving husband, my three beautiful children, my friends and family. Most of all to my best friend. Thanks to everyone for believing in me and my dreams. To my readers, thank you for your love and support. Special thank you to Dalexrs for their editorial services.

Table of Contents

Chapter One

It's Friday night and five friends sit around the table at their favorite bar having a great time celebrating. On this night, the bar had a good crowd with good music and there was a lot of single ladies there who were looking for a good time. Leo looks up and signals the waitress to bring more drinks to the table for him and his friends. A few minutes later the waitress brings the group their drinks. Leo, Craig, Marcus, Sam, and Jerry raise their bottles and cheers with excitement, slamming their beer bottles together celebrating Sam's divorce. The friends are in a drunken state, laughing hysterically, as they vow to each other that no one in the group will ever get married again. Throughout the night the men continued celebrating Sam's new freedom.

Sam was married to his wife for only three weeks then she decided that their marriage was not going to work. Sam, the quiet one in the group, would do anything for his friends especially his best friend Leo. Sam's wife could not understand the magnitude of their strange relationship, and this made her unhappy. Leo loved Sam like a brother, there was nothing that they would not do for each other. Leo was the strongest one in the group and his friends called him "The Lion" due to his protective nature, aggression, and anger.

Craig, Jerry, and Marcus are known to be the party boys of the group. These three have been sharing the same apartment since their college days and have no plans of ever growing up. These party boys decided that college was not for them and after one year in college they join the military. During boot camp, they met Leo and Sam. One day during a training exercise, Sam was singled out and Leo, Marcus, Jerry, and Craig came to his defense. Due to the nature of their aggression, they were all discharge from the military. This did not bother them and over the years the five men became the best of friends and formed their own team.

A few tables behind the men, Leanna celebrates her new promotion as the Regional Store Manager with her four best friends. This was Leanna's first time going to a bar and she did not want to disappoint her friends. Looking around at the scantily clad women that mirrored her friends, she suddenly felt unsure about her attire. Leanna wore her fitted black jeans, a simple white blouse, and a black jacket. Getting dressed, she thought she selected an outfit that stated "sexy, young, professional" but now she worried, she may have missed the mark.

Leanna was a loner, shy, and very fragile. The bar was too crowded for her, and this was not the place she wanted to be on a Friday night. Leanna had an older sister Anna, who was the more adventurous one. Even though Anna is four years older than Leanna they are often mistaken for twins. Anna spends most of her time traveling the world, she likes to get out and really see the world while Leanna would rather stay at home and read about it. Anna was more outgoing, friendly, and open to try exciting new things. She was everything that Leanna wanted to be with Anna gone on her adventures. Leanna had no choice but to spend most of her time with her friends Sara, Tracy, Laura, and Michelle. Over the years, Leanna's friends embolden her to try new things this gave Leanna the confidence that she needs. With the support of her college friends Leanna felt good about trying new things this led to them became best friends.

Tonight, the ladies made it their life mission to find the virgin Leanna the man of her dreams. Tracy starts to check out the men in the bar, while the rest of her friends makes fun of the men as they walked past their table. Tracy could tell by Leanna's facial expression that she wanted to leave the bar. She leans over to Leanna, "Come on Leanna, pick the man of your dreams." Leanna sits quietly as she looks at her watered-down drink. Sara looks over at Leanna's drink, "We're going to need more drinks to liven up this party."

Sara rushes over to the bar counter yelling, "One more round of drinks for my girls!" Sara was the life of the party and in no time, she grabs the attention of the men in the bar. As if on que, Craig quickly approaches Sara and engages in a little friendly conversation with her. Sara's was being overly friendly to Craig, and this was a concern for Laura, Michelle, Tracy, and Leanna as they rushed over to rescue Sara. Marcus gets up and welcome the ladies, warmly introducing his friends to them. Sara leans over to Craig, she takes the cherry from his drink and eats it "What are you guys up too tonight?" She flips her hair as she leans in closer to Craig. Craig looks over at Sam who stumbles as he tries to stand up. With a muted thud, thanks to the loud music, Sam falls off his chair as Jerry struggles to help him up.

Craig slides over closer to Sara. He slowly tucks her hair behind her ear as he whispers, "We are celebrating our boys' Sam's divorce." Jerry drunkenly gets up from his chair, "To Sam for leaving that cheating wicked witch from the west." The bartender approaches with the drinks Sara ordered. Feeling generous, Michelle orders a round of drinks for the men in support of their celebration. Craig asks Sara and her friends to join them. The new friends pull their tables and chairs together as they talk and get to know each other. After a few more drinks, the men started to pair up with the ladies.

Craig and Sara were getting very close; kissing the palm of her hand as he led her to the dance floor. Michelle looks over at Sara and Craig as they dance and smiled. Marcus, noticing her smiling, he gently helps Michelle up to her feet. "Let's dance," he says. Michelle looks in his eyes and the two went to the dance floor. Laura eyeballed Jerry as he tries to hold her hand, she pulls away from him as they walked to the dance floor, arguing the entire time. Tracy felt sorry for Sam, as he plays the victim in his divorce. She comforts him, promising that she would take care of him as they stumbled to the dance floor. Sam looks back at Leo and smiled, he gives Leo two thumbs up.

Leo laughs at Sam as Leanna sat quietly across from him. Leo and Leanna look over at their friends, shaking their heads with disbelief as they watch the spectacle unfold before them. Their friends are on the dancefloor dancing offbeat and falling all over each other. Leanna shyly glances over at Leo. She slowly takes a sip of her water-down drink. This was the first time she has ever seen a man as tall and built like him. Leo notices that Leanna was looking at him. He sits up straight, he reaches for his drink, chugging the entire glass of beer. Leanna watches him closely with enchantment as they both could feel the chemistry between them. Leanna was shy and Leo notices her shyness. He looks at her as she struggles to keep her hair out of her face. She had a full head of curls that often acted as if they had a mind of their own.

Leo leans over to her resting his arm on the table "I love your hair." Leanna looks up into Leo eyes as she continues to struggle with her curly hair as it falls in her face. Leo gently smiles at Leanna as he sits back in his chair. She could feel the warmth of her blood rushing throughout her body. Leo gazes into Leanna's eyes knowing that they both felt the desire for each other.

Moving closer to Leanna, the two began to talk about their work, family, and hobbies. Leo tells Leanna about his brief time in the military and his construction business. Leanna askes Leo more about his construction business and listens with great fascination. She stares into his brown eyes, enchanted when he speaks. Leanna fell under his spell, hypnotized by her desires.

As their friends dance the night away, Leo and Leanna got to know each other on a more personal level. Leo was nine years older than Leanna and he was very handsome. He could have any women in the room, but he wanted Leanna. Leanna could tell that life has not been kind to him. Even though Leo was very handsome, he had a rough look to him. Despite the hint of danger, when he speaks Leanna quivers with lust.

Leanna tells Leo about her estranged older sister that lives in Japan, and about her mom who retired shortly after her dad died. Leo knew that family can be somewhat challenging as he tells her about his brother. As they continued to get to know one another, the connection they had seemed to be almost spiritual, transcending time and space. Connecting on a spiritual level, Leo has never felt this kind of connection before. Intrigued by this, he observers her body language he could see how gentile and fragile Leanna was. Leo wonders if he was falling in love with Leanna or would it be just another one-night stand.

At closing time, the mixologist tells Jerry "Wrap it up, we're closing it's time to go." Jerry looks over at the crowded bar "we'll leave when they leave" he continues to dance with Michelle. The mixologist signals the DJ to stop the music. With no more grooves spilling from the speakers, the crowd started to make their way to the front of the bar. Leo was not happy with this. He gets up and yells, "Come on, one more round!" He raised his arm in defiance, a gesture that accidently elbows another guy in the face. With the quickest of reflexes, the guy punches Leo in the chest, but missing the second swing, hits Jerry in the face.

This led to a massive bar fight between Leo's group and the other guy's group. A waitress runs to the phone frantically, calling the police to report the fight. The once happy atmosphere of the bar descended into utter chaos. As the crowd jumps in, kicking and punching the men, Leo grabs his accidental opponent, using him to push the crowd to the front door and out of the bar as they fought, keeping the crowd away from Leanna.

The police sirens and flashing lights came closer and closer to the front

of the bar. The crowd started to run in opposite directions. Leo was on top of the guy as they were rolling around fighting in the grass. Leanna runs over as she tries to grab Leo; she rips his shirt as she tries to pull Leo off the guys. "Leo let's go!" Leanna pleaded desperately while pulling at his shirt with all her might. Leo gets up and kicks the guy. Spitting out blood, defiantly, the guy yells,

"Listen to your bitch!" Leo kicks him again. Leanna finally manages to pull Leo away and she hastily leads Leo to her car. "Leo come on, let's go", said Leanna, not noticing her phone as it falls out of her pocket and into the overgrown grass.

As they reach the car, she laughs nervously, "You're crazy, get it, get in." as they both enter the car. Leanna drives off in the opposite direction of the police. That night Leanna took the long way home as she laughs and talk about fight. Leanna looks over at Leo, "This was not the girl's night I was promised, that guy was crazy!" Leo laughs at how scared Leanna was as she frantically drives looking behind her. Leo sighs, "I guess I owe you a second date." Leanna looks over at Leo and smiles as she thinks of the possibility of seeing him again. As they drove, Leo did not recognize the area. "Where are we going?", he asks. Leanna turns and looks at him, "I don't know I'm just driving. I don't live too far from here though." Leo looks out the car window and up at the stars, "Let's go to your house." She lifted an eyebrow, "I don't think that is a good idea."

Leanna did not think it was a good idea to bring a man that she has known for a few hours to her home. She continues to drive around the city. The more they talked the more Leanna felt at ease with Leo. Not knowing what to do she continues to drive nervously, as she talks about her new job position. She looks over at Leo as he slowly nobs off to sleep Leanna decides to head home. After driving around, the city for an hour before she pulls into the long driveway. As soon as Leanna cut the engine off, Leo hopped out of the car. He walks around the front of the car as Leanna watches him skeptically, and he opened the door for Leanna. This is different, she thinks to herself. She looks up at Leo announcing, "Here we are!" getting out of the car, fumbling through her handbag for her keys. They approached the door, and she struggles to unlock it. Leo smiles as he stares at her, "You need some help?" Ignoring him, Leanna forces the door open, and they walk inside. She points to the left, "The guest bedroom is down the hall; you're welcome to stay the night." Leo looks to his left as he slowly checks out Leanna's home, "Nice place, thanks."

Leanna puts her keys on the key holder and takes her jacket off. She looks at Leo's bruised and swollen face, "If you want, I can get some ice on that?", she said, gesturing towards his face. Leo touches his chin, "I would like that." As they enter the kitchen, Leo looks around, "Where is the bathroom?" Leanna points to the guest bedroom. Leo walks down the hall, makes a left into the bedroom, and uses the bathroom. He turns on the water, Leanna stood quietly in the hallway just outside the bedroom door as she listens intensively.

After washing his face, Leo turns off the water. Leanna rushes to the kitchen turning on all the lights. With a smile on her face, she quickly grabs a Ziploc bag and puts some ice in it. Leo walks back into the kitchen taking off his grass stained, ripped up shirt. Leanna stares at his built frame, as he towers over her, shirtless. He pulls out the chair and sits down around the kitchen table.

Leanna walks over to him, placing the ice pack on his cheek. She looks at his pink, wet, lips with lust in her eyes. He grabs her hand and Leanna jumps. Her heart skips a beat as he slowly moves her hand towards his chin. He looks into Leanna's dark brown eyes, "My chin hurts more." He firmly holds her tiny hand to his chin. Leanna was not sure of his actions, and she quickly pulled her hand away shakily she takes a few steps back. Leo could see that she was scared and unsure of his actions. He smiles at her reassuringly, "Thank you." Leanna notices that it was almost morning, and she did not want him to leave, "I can make us some breakfast if you're hungry." she said shyly.

Leo leaned over to her and whispered, "Yes, I'm so hungry." Leanna walks timidly over to the refrigerator, opens the door, and gets the eggs. She was nervous as they talked about her favorite breakfast and their childhood, but she soon became at ease as she expertly navigated the kitchen cooking, as the space was filled with the savory smells of breakfast. Leo closely watches her with thoughts of kissing her lips. He was captivated by her natural beauty, her lips as she spoke, her long wild hair and the way it curls.

Leanna could feel Leo watching her as she put her massive curly hair up in a loose bun. Leo notices the moon shape birthmark on her neck. Feeling his gaze, she stumbled over her words trying to remember what she was talking about. Leo smiles knowingly at her. He has never felt this way before he thinks to himself, watching her with intensity. Leo sits back in his chair as Leanna bites her lips while she cuts the strawberries for his pancakes.

That morning Leanna made eggs, beacon, and pancakes for breakfast. Enough food to feed ten men and Leo enjoyed every bite. Once they got through eating breakfast, Leanna and Leo cleaned up the kitchen as if they've done this before. Leo sits on the couch and Leanna offers him a glass of wine. He asked Leanna to join him on the couch, there they sit and talk for hours. With the rising of the sun Leanna jumped up, "Good night, Leo."

Leo stood up shirtless, towering over her. Looking into her eye, he lifts her chin and gently kisses her lips. Leanna could feel the warmth of his lips on hers and she pulls him in closer. He moves his hands slowly as grabs her buttocks and lifts her closer to him. She wraps her legs around his waist as he carries her to the bedroom. Leo laid her down gently on the bed kissing her lips. He stops and looks into her dark brown eyes, "Do you want me to stop?" Leanna leans in closer to him, "No, don't stop." She pulls him in closer kissing his lips as he undresses her slowly. She looks into Leo's eyes, "I don't know what to do... I've never... This is my first time." Leo gently kisses her lips. He kisses gently on her neck and her breasts. As she quivers, his lips move lower and lower. He gets lost as he tastes her flower. Leanna moans as she trembles with pleasure. Leo reaches over and covers Leanna's mouth as he gently opens her flower for the first time. That night Leo and Leanna made love. For Leanna this was her first time. For Leo, the untamable lion, he was falling in love.

As Leanna slept, Leo slowly gets up and goes to the bathroom to get dressed. He takes a long look at himself in the bathroom mirror. Leo takes his cellphone out of his pocket and looks at the time. It was 3:17 pm when Leo was dressed and ready to leave. He slowly opens the bathroom door and looks over at Leanna as she slept. He stood quietly in the doorway of the bathroom and watches Leanna sleeping on the bed. He thinks about the amazing night that they had together. The connection they have, he could not bear the thought of hurting her. In that moment, Leo made the decision to stay. As he climbs back into bed, Leanna reaches over and pulls him closer to her. Leo Laid in bed with his eyes open as Leanna slept in his arms.

A few hours later Leanna woke up, she looks over smiling at Leo as he slept by her. Her mouth got watery as she stares at his massive biceps and his lips as he slept. This was all new to Leanna. She had never been with anyone before, and she did not want their time together to come to an end. Leanna slows crawls out of the bed, she quietly pulls out a summer dress from the dresser draw. She quickly dresses, leaving her over-sized shirt on the bed for Leo. Then she sneaks off to the kitchen to make dinner for two.

Leo opens his glazed sleepy eyes. He sees Leanna as she quietly tries to sneak out the room. He gets up and puts on the guinea tee that Leanna left on the bed for him. Then he walks to the kitchen and is greeted by the sight of Leanna dancing with excitement while she prepares dinner. He leans on the wall and watches her for a moment. He was hypnotized by her natural beauty as he thinks about last night. Leo walks into to the kitchen, as his eyes sliding down her body, he leans over and kisses her.

After a great weekend together, the time came for Leo to go home. Leanna felt like she was never going see him again. She slowly walks him to the door. Leo kisses her good-bye, and she watches as he strolls to Sam's car. Leanna sadly closes the door as he disappeared inside Sam's car, but once inside the house she jumps on the couch dancing with glee, not knowing that Leo and Sam could see her through the window.

On the ride home Leo called Marcus and tells him about his weekend with Leanna. Leo could not get Leanna out of his head. He kept thinking about their weekend together. He calls Leanna but the phone line was busy. He tries a few more times but the line was still busy. He was wondering if he was calling the wrong number, but he continues to call hoping that Leanna will answer the phone.

Chapter Two

Leanna franticly searches her car and home for her phone. Unable to find it, she started to cry at the thought of missing Leo's call.

Leo continued to call Leanna throughout the day and all his calls went unanswered. Leo started to think that Leanna had blew him off. He tries to remember her home address. Flustered, he calls Sam who, big surprise, was no help to him.

Leo when to work late that day after spending the entire morning thinking about Leanna and calling her. On his way to work Leo kept daydreaming about Leanna. As he replays the image of them making love, he smiles. Leo gets lost in his thoughts, as he thinks of the sweet taste of her flower, the warmth of her touch, and the curve of her body. He slowly pulls in his parking space at work and hops out of his truck. As the warmth of the sun hit his skin he smiled. Craig hurried over to him and hands him a cup of coffee, "Where the hell have you been? Wipe that stupid look off your face."

Leo laughs at Craig, he reaches for the coffee "I'm the boss, I can be late" as they walk into the building. Leo looks over at Jerry sitting at his desk. Jerry looks up and sees Leo walking towards his office. "Sprung!" Jerry yells, getting up and breaking into a jog to Leo's office. Craig sees him coming and slams the door in his face. Craig sat on the chair in Leo's office and started to drill him for more information about his weekend with Leanna. He stares at Leo, "Was she good?" Leo shakes his head as he ignores Craig's question.

Jerry barges into Leo's office, falling to his knees, begging Leo to tell him about his weekend. Leo could not hold it in anymore, he gave in and told his friends that Leanna was amazing. This information was not enough for Jerry and Craig, they continued to drill Leo for the raw details. Leo sighs as he turns in his chair. He looks at his friends with a sneaky smile on his face, "It was her first time." They erupt in howls of victory and laughter. Craig joins Jerry on the floor with excitement, as the two clowns dramatically worship Leo the lion.

Leo asked Jerry about his weekend. Jerry shakes his head, "Man… you're lucky. Leanna's friend Laura, that bitch is crazy." He lifts his shirt and shows Leo and Craig his back. "She tied me up and beat me. Look at my back! I'm scared for life." Jerry looked genuinely concerned, Leo and Craig laughed at Jerry as he sits on the edge of the Leo's desk having flashbacks. "It's not funny, she beat me with a belt! She's fine as hell though," said Jerry looking defeated. Leo and Craig continue to laugh at Jerry; he got mad at his friends and stormed out of the office. Back at his desk, Jerry sneaks and call Laura asking if he could see her again.

Leo went about his workday continuously checking his phone to see if Leanna had returned his calls. At work, Leanna made a quick call to order a new phone. She requested for the phone be delivered to her home by the end of the day. Sara franticly calls Leanna at work, "We've been calling you, are you okay? Oh my God Leo is so hot, tell me everything that happened," she said eagerly. Leanna walked to her office for some privacy she gently closed the door. Fill with the excitement of the weekend she tells Sara about Leo and their magical weekend together. Sara was so excited for Leanna as she yells for Michelle to come to her office.

Michelle and Sara convinced Leanna that Leo was into her and encouraging Leanna to call Leo and confess how she truly felt about him. Leanna boss walks into her office and she ended their phone call.

Everyone went on with their normal daily routine not knowing that the bar fight left one man named Mark hospitalized.

Mark was a well-known drunk and he later died due to his health and alcohol intake. Mark's older brother Luke was told the sad news of the death of his younger brother. Luke was mad and Mark's wife convinced him that Mark died due to the fight. With revenge in his heart, Luke left New York for Georgia in a hurry. He wanted the man who killed his brother to pay with his life.

Luke was not stranger to violence as a child his father would take him and his brother to visit their uncle on the farm to hunt. These visitations will conclude with their father teaching his two sons how to carve. Their canvas of choice was young women and men. Luke served seven years in prison for murdering a young couple while they were on vacation in the mountains. His father was able to buy Luke's freedom whenever he would commit these violent acts. For the past year he has been in hiding and is currently wanted for questioning on the disappearance of several college girls.

Luke was able to buy his way, and when he arrived in town, the first place he went was the bar. He sees some construction going on at the entrance of the bar. He walks over to the site, "What happened to the door?", Luke says to himself. He walks to the front of the building, observing all the angles as he looks for cameras. He walked over to the grass looking at the other buildings for any cameras that may have recorded the fight. Luke steps on Leanna's phone, he looks down and picks up the phone hiding the phone in his jacket.

In a haste he left the bar and walked around the downtown area looking for a motel for the night. Luke comes across some abandoned undeveloped home on a deserted street. He breaks in the abandoned home as he walks through the house, he looks around to make sure that the house was empty. He sits on the floor gazing out the window he notices two beautiful women as they walk done the deserted street. Watching them as they slowly walk passes the gate, he takes the phone out of his jacket and looks at his reflection on the broken phone screen.

He looks at the water-damaged device and decided to unlock the phone. After a few hours, Luke was able to unlock it. He went through Leanna's phone looking at her personal photo albums. He checks Leanna's messages and decides to track her down. He opens the map app and could see all the places that she's been. He spent the rest of the day following her. Leanna did not do much that day and he decided that she had nothing to do with the death of his brother's death. Luke decides to do some more investigating and follow other leads, but first he needed to meet with his cousin Michael.

Later that night Leo decided to show up to Leanna's home since he did not hear from her, and he desperately wanted to see her again. Leanna was still trying to figure out how to link her old phone to her new cell phone when she heard the doorbell. She rushes to the window, wondering who that could be at this hour of the night. Leanna was full of excitement to see Leo standing there with a lost look at his face. Leo thought that he was at the wrong house as he looks around, he did not recognize the area. He was about to leave then Leanna rushes to open the door smiling at Leo, he hugs her, and she invites him in and offers him a beer.

Leo felt a strong connection to Leanna, but he was unsure if she wanted to be with someone like him. They sat on the couch and talked for hours. Leo became more open about his feelings for Leanna. Leanna confesses her feelings to Leo, and he was so happy that she felt the same way. He takes Leanna's hands in his, kissing them as he confesses his love for her. Leanna's phone rings and she gets up and runs to the room to answer her phone. It was Laura and Michelle on the phone. Leanna told her friends that Leo was in the next room. Michelle, filled with excitement, "OH MY GOD…. Girl you better ride that mountain man!" Laura yells at the phone, "Do that thing I showed you in college." Leanna closes her room door and whispers into the phone, "I am not. you guys are so nasty... plus I like this guy." Leo walks over and knocks on the room door, "Do you need me to come back some other time?"

Leanna rushes her friends off the phone, and she opens the door for Leo, "No." She jumps on him and kisses him; he picks her up into his arms. That night they make passionate love, and this time Leanna did not hold back. She took charge doing everything her friends told her to do and Leo loved every minute of it as he embraced the moment. Their passion for each other burns throughout the night.

As the weeks went by, Leo started to spend most of his nights with Leanna, but this was not enough for her. One morning as Leo got ready for work, Leanna walks over to him and hands him his coffee. She puts her head on his chest, "You should move in so that you can be closer to work." Leo quickly greed and the new couple started to plan their new living arrangements together. A few weeks later with the help of their friends the new couple was all moved in. As the months go by, Leo and Leanna's passion for each other grow stronger. Their home was filled with joy, friends, family, love, and laughter.

One day, at work, Leanna fell ill, and she decides to go to the Emergency room. Leanna sat there as she nervously answers the physician's questions about her sex life and partners. The physician checked Leanna and requested some blood from her to confirm his suspicions. A few minutes later, nurse Rebecca walked in the room with the results, "Your blood work confirms that you are six to eight weeks pregnant," she said smiling.

Leanna sat there in shock and confusion. She confessed to the nurse about Leo and how they met at the bar. She told the nurse about the fight and now she's going to have Leo's baby. Leanna was shocked that this was all happening so fast. She was worried about telling Leo the news. Leanna laid on the bed for a while, exhausted from thinking about how she was going to break the news to Leo.

Meanwhile, the nurse remembered that her boyfriend's cousin died due to injuries from a bar fight. As Leanna got dressed, the nurse rushes to the phone and called her boyfriend Michael. She tells him about Leanna and her story about the fight at the bar. Michael instructs Rebecca to follow Leanna and to call him if she sees Leo. As Leanna waits for her discharge papers at the nursing station, Rebecca faked being ill, and she was sent home for the day. Rebecca got in her car and followed Leanna home keeping her distance. On the way home Leanna called Tracy and told her to call everyone. With all her friends on the phone Leanna told them the good news. As they screamed with excitement, they encouraged Leanna to call Leo and tell him. Leanna was scared to call Leo but ensured her friends that she would tell him tonight when he gets home.

Leanna pulls into her driveway and Rebecca started to record Leanna as she enters her home. After obtaining her footage, Rebecca rushed home and is greeted by Luke as soon as she walks through the front door. She begins to tell Luke and Michael about Leanna and her story. Hearing this news, they were all convinced that Leanna's boyfriend killed Mark. Luke walked over to the window and closes the blinds. He looks up at Mark's photo on the wall, "I'll make him pay for this, I promise you," he says with calm anger. Luke told Michael and Rebecca that, "he will take it from here" and he left his cousin's home.

Leanna waited anxiously by the door for Leo to come home as she tries to come up with different ways of telling him that she is pregnant. Leo trucks pulls in the long driveway and Leanna sees the truck's headlights. She rushes to open the door as he parked the truck. Leo walks in and kisses her, "You look worried, what's going on, are you okay, are you hurt?" Leanna was scared to tell Leo. She did not want to lose him. Most of all she did not know how he would react to the news.

Leanna takes a few steps backwards, stopped and looks up at Leo with tears in her eyes. "I'm pregnant Leo!" she said, full of emotion as her tears run down her cheeks. Leo slowly walks up to Leanna. He looks at her, holds her hands in disbelief, "You're pregnant? I'm going to be a dad?" he says in quiet surprise. He grabs Leanna and kisses her with excitement, celebrating the new addition to the family he embraces her. With this news Leo was ready to take the next step. He looks into Leanna's eyes as her tears run down her cheeks. Leo wipes her tears, "Leanna, marry me?" he asks lovingly.

Leanna wipes her tears, "What? Yes, yes, I'll marry you," she says, her heart feeling full. As the happy couple shares their news with family and friends, they began to prepare their home for the arrival of their baby. Luke watches the happy couple from a distance, planning his revenge, and he decided it was time to make his move.

A few weeks later Leo was on his way to work in heavy rain when a truck starts to follow him with bright blinding lights. Leo tries to get over as the truck mirrors his every move. The white truck backs off as Leo pulls over to the slow lane, getting stuck behind a six-wheeler cargo truck. Leo waits to get off on the next exit, then the driver of the white pickup truck speeds up heading straight for Leo's truck. Leo saw that the truck was driving at a fast speed and out of control. He pulled to the right, hastily getting off the interstate as the truck continued to speed up out of control.

Thinking nothing of this, Leo went on about his day at work, happily telling his friends at about Leanna's strange cravings. As the weeks passed by Leanna's belly began to show. Leanna decides to send and thank you card and a gift basket to the physician and the staff at the hospital. The security guard delivery the basket to the nurse's station and Rebecca signed for the gift basket.

She looks at the card and saw that the gift was from Leanna and Leo. She walks over to the trash can and discarded the basket and the thank you card. Rebecca went back to her desk and accesses Leanna's medical health records. She was able to calculate that Leanna was four months pregnant. Rebecca was unable to conceived and she grew jealous of Leanna and her pregnancy. Filled with jealousy she calls Luke, "Luke you are not a good brother, you have not kept your promise to Mark." Her words cutting him to the core she hangs up the phone on him. With Rebecca's words still ringing in his head, Luke decided it was time to make his moves to honor his brother and his promise.

One afternoon Leanna came home from work early as she prepared dinner for Leo. She realized she was missing a few items. Leanna called Leo but got his voice mail. Leo had left his phone to charge in his work truck at the construction site. Later that night Leo gets home late, and Leanna greeted him at the door as she was leaving to go to the store.

He reaches to hug her, and she pushes him away, "Leo you stink," she says, scrunching her nose in playful disgust. Leo leans over and kisses her, "You love my smell," he kisses her again and kisses her growing belly. Leo rushes to the bathroom taking off his clothing. He turns on the shower, "hey...Leanna... wait for me I'll go with you." She searches her handbag for her keys. "It's okay," she yells, "I won't be long." Leanna sees her keys on the table. She walks over and picks them up, then walks out of the house. Leanna turned around to go back in the house, realizing she forgot the shopping list.

Luke saw her and in the next moment, he grabbed her, forcing Leanna into his car. With his hand covering her mouth she was unable to scream. That night Luke took Leanna to the old, abandoned house that he was living in. There he ties her up and records her as he scares her and threaten her life. He showed Leanna her old cell phone then he empties her handbag on the floor. He picks up her new cell phone and brings it to Leanna, forcing her to unlock it.

Leo steps out the shower, reaching for his towel, he walks to the bedroom. He picks up his cell phone to check Leanna's location. Leanna's location sharing had ended. In a panic he called her. The phone rings and rings. Leanna tries to break loose from her restraints to get to the phone. Luke grabs her face, "I'm going to cut that pretty face so that no one will recognize you," he says with so much malice Leanna could feel her blood stand still. Meanwhile, Leo quickly runs out the front door, outside looking for Leanna. Her car was there but Leanna was not. Leo hangs up the phone and calls Leanna again, this time Luke answer her phone.

Leo was shocked to hear a man on the other end of the phone. Shock turned to terror when he hears Leanna in the background weeping and begging. Leo begins to beg for Leanna to be released and for him to take her place. Luke coldly laughed at Leo, "I'm going to take everything from you." The phone line went dead. Luke grabs Leanna's face, he licks her face, as she tries to pull away from him. He grabs her firmly, as he smells her hair, he whispers to her, "I've been watching you and wanting you," he stares manically into her eyes.

Luke unlocks Leanna's phone, he calls Leo. Leo in disbelief was franticly screams at his phone then he sees the incoming video call coming from Leanna's phone. He quickly answers his phone. Luke shared a live video. Now Leo was face to face with is worst nightmare, as he witnesses Luke's evil acts. Luke violently rips off Leanna's clothing, exposing her breasts and her fragile growing belly. He carves his name on her belly, then he pushes her over to the table. He bends her over the table he reaches up her dress, ripping off her underwear and assaulted her. Luke sets down the phone as he continues to share the live video himself assaulting Leanna. Then he grabbed Leanna by the neck and choked her until she was unconscious. Leo watches with rage as he sees Luke's sick and violent acts. Then Luke picks up the phone and smiled at Leo as he ended the video sharing.

Chapter Three

Leo franticly called the police to report Leanna's kidnapping and assault. The cops come to their home as the investigators asks Leo a few questions. Leo sat on the couch with a void look on his face as his friend Jerry offered him kind words of encouragement. Leo got mad at the investigator for questioning him instead of sending people from their team to go look for Leanna. He attacks the investigator as he was going through Leanna's personal belongings.

Leanna's friends, Tracy, Michelle, and Sara stayed in the kitchen making posters while Laura calls the local hospitals to see if anyone fitting Leanna's description was there. They worked diligently making calls, leaving messages, and asking friends and family if they had seen or heard from Leanna. Three days later as Leo sits by the phone his friend Sam observed him from a distance. While Jerry makes them lunch, Sam got up and walked over to Leo, "We going to find her, and the bastard that did this to you." Just then, Leo's cell phone rings and it was Laura on the phone. She was crying, "Leo, someone fitting Leanna's description was found in the south parking lot of the hospital."

Leo, Jerry, and Sam rushes to the hospital. Craig and Marcus met them at the door as they ran through the emergency department of the hospital. In front of room number seven, Leo sees Leanna's mother sitting on the chair weeping, broken hearted as Sara, Michelle, Tracy, and Laura were on their knees crying weeping on the floor by her feet. They hold each other as the doctor walks over to them "I'm sorry we did everything that we could do, they are gone." Leo rushes over to the doctor grabbing the doctor's jacket as he falls to the floor, his friend Sam rushed over to comfort him. Leanna was gone and so was their unborn child. Luke had taken Leo's world away. There was nothing left for Leo to live for. Leo gets up and ran to Leanna's room as his anger grows into rage. He looks at Leanna's fragile, unrecognizable, lifeless body. He walks over to his son. The level of pain on Leo's face was raw and everyone could feel his heartbreak. Sam and Jerry were immediately at their friend's side to pull him out of the room. The sight was too much for Leo to bare, he ran out of the hospital. Running through the parking lot, he fell to his knees in the rain as he shrieks with the rolling thunder. Leo's friends rush to the parking lot as he continues to shriek in the rain; the men tried to help him to his feet. With brute strength Leo pushes his friends off him. That night, a part of Leo died.

Two weeks goes by as Leanna and her son get ready to be laid to rest. In Leo's mind, the vile vision of what Luke did to Leanna played repeatedly. He could hear Leanna's screaming every time he closes his eyes, he could see her dismantled face and there was nothing he could have done differently to save her.

Leo felt that he had failed to protect Leanna and now she was gone forever. He sat quietly on the edge of his chair, lost in his thoughts during Leanna's services. As the pastor begins to speak Leo closed his eyes, he could see Leanna smiling at him. He could hear her laughing at his jokes, he visualizes his son's tiny finger playing in Leanna's beautiful unruly hair while she's nursing him.

He could smell Leanna's perfume as the wind blows. Leo opened his eyes then reality set in. He knew that this was all gone. Luke has taken this from him. Later that night, at Leo and Leanna's home. Friends and family sat in the family room as they share their memories of Leanna. Her friends talk about their college days, how they met her, and her new promotion. Sara reminded Leo of the endless love that Leanna had for him. Leanna's aging mother cries for her daughter, wishing that Leanna's sister Anna was there to comfort her. Crying, she turns and looks over at Leo as he sat on the edge of the couch.

Leo had his head down, he could not get the image of his beloved Leanna's lifeless body, her wounds, and his son in her arms out of his head. This was too much for Leo to handle. He rushes to the front door slamming it behind him. Sam ran outside following Leo down the long driveway, "Leo, where are you going? I'm coming with you," Sam said as he opens the car door, fearing what Leo might do. Sam hopped in the driver seat as Leo sat in the passenger seat of his work truck. The two men sit in silence. Sam drove for an hour unsure of where they were going. Leo looks ahead at the exit sign, he tells Sam, "Get off here on this exit, and take me to the police station." Sam did what he was told. At the police station, Leo requested to see the full report on Leanna's case from the detective. He refused to give it to him and sent them home. Back at the house Jerry, Marcus, and Craig anxiously waited for them to return wondering what was taking them so long.

Marcus went outside and he saw Leo's truck as it turned onto their street. As the truck approaches the house, he met them in the driveway. As they walk into the house Sam sat down and began to tell them what happened at the police station. Craig kicks the pillow that was on the floor. Jerry moves out of the way of the pillow. Jerry not being a fan of the justice system makes it clear they did not need the police to help them. He approaches Leo, "Man... I can call Carlos. I'm sure he can hack in their system and get the files." Leo looks at Jerry with rage in his eyes, "Yes, call Carlos and see what he can do."

Jerry reaches for his cell phone and makes the call. Carlos was at home with his family, playing with his children on their gaming system when a call from an unknown number came up on his computer. He rushes his son out the room and gave his wife their baby. He locks the door as he enters his password and access codes on the keyboard. "Yo, this is C the line is clear. Jerry how you been man? Dang it's been a minute man. Sorry I missed Sam's divorce party." he said as he adjusted his headset over his ears. Carlos was filled excitement to hear from Jerry as he asked about the crew. Jerry sighs, "Carlos what was the last thing you said to me?" Carlos exhales slowly, "Only call me if you need me."

Jerry told Carlos the bad news about Leanna, and Carlos was more than happy to hack in the police station computer system and get a copy of the files. In minutes Carlos was able to access Leanna's case file. He printed the files to Leo's personal home printer. Carlos could see the police report and he could feel Leo's pain. He knew that he needed to be with his team.

Carlos gets off the phone with Jerry. He sat there for a while reading the reports, he decided that he needed to be with his friends. He walks over to his wife, as she feeds their young daughter, he tells her the bad news. His wife was concerned about Leo, and she encourages Carlos to make the trip. Carlos knew what could happen if he goes. He kisses his wife on the head, "They would do the same for me in a heartbeat." he whispers to her.

Carlos kisses his family, and he left his home in Mexico and headed to Atlanta. During the flight Carlos looks at his bible as he prays, he kisses his cross. He pulls out an old photo of his friends that he uses as a book marker. He smiles as he remembers the good old days in the marines with his unit. He puts the photo back between the pages of his bible and closes his eyes.

Marcus stood by the printer waiting for the files to print. Just then Leo walks over to him, and the two men wait impatiently for the large file to print. Images of Leanna's body and the notes of what was done to her started pouring out from the machine almost as angrily as Leo felt. Words like beaten, rape, choked, and carvings was too much for Leo to relive. He screamed with rage as his anger grew. Craig snatched the papers from Leo hands. He turns to him, "Leo, what do you need us to do? Just say it, and we'll do it."

Leo paces the floor in Leanna's office, he stopped and looks up at the wall he reaches for the photo of Leanna holding her belly. He puts the photo back on the wall he turns and looks at his friends crossing his arms, "I want him to feel what I am feeling, then I want to bathe in his blood," he says angrily. With that, Sam, Marcus, Craig, and Jerry stood up. Sam starts to yell out a list of items that the team will need for this job. Knowing their assignments and duties, the men got in their cars and went shopping for the supplies. They traveled to several supply stores, staying out of view from the cameras. Sam also went and got some supplies from Leo's construction business.

With all the supplies collected they headed back to Leo's house. The men started to pack up their gear when Carlos rang the doorbell. Jerry opens the door as the men stand closely behind him. They're Carlos stood smiling at Jerry, "Sorry I didn't get here sooner," he said with a concern tone. Carlos walks in as Sam, Craig, and Marcus greeted him. He walks up to Leo, "I'm truly sorry man." Leo looks up at Carlos as he gets up and hugs his old friend.

Jerry throws a bag of supplies at Carlos and soon the men left Leo's home in a hurry. Carlos and Jerry rode with Craig while Marcus and Sam rode with Leo. The men check into a rundown motel and Marcus pays more than the cost, all in cash; the clerk did not ask any questions. As Marcus and Jerry checks out the rooms. Outside, Craig and Sam walk the perimeter of the motel, looking for the location of the security cameras.

As the six friends gather in Leo's the motel room, Carlos opens his bag and pulls out a small black box. In the box he had a black cross neckless for Jerry, and a pair of black matching earrings for Marcus. Carlos walked over to Leo and gave him a black bracelet with a lion on it. Sam was impressed with Leo's gift, he waited patiently for his gift. Carlos slowly walked over to Sam and gave him a black watch. Sam examines the watch, "It's broken," he said while holding it up to his ear, Sam taps on the screen of the watch, realizing the next level technology. Carlos helps him to adjust the watch. Craig walks over to admire Sam's gift nodding with approval. Carlos smiled at him and handed him a black lighter.

The friends sat on the floor in the motel room, and they began to finalize their plan. Carlos logged on to his computer and connects it to the television in the motel room. Carlos begins to drill

Leo on the night Leanna died. The more questions Carlos asked Leo, the more upset Leo got. Frustrated, Leo gets up he walked over to the table and made himself a drink. He takes a sip of his drink and remember the white pickup truck that almost ran him off the road.

Leo takes another sip of his drink. He sits his cup on the table he looks over at Carlos, "Carlos can you hack into the police system and see if there was any reports or accidents involving a white pickup truck?" Being the tech guy of the group Carols was able to hack into the police system in minutes. Carlos intensely strolls through the pages of the reports. He leans closer to the laptop's monitor, "There was a call reporting a truck driving out of control. The truck is registered to a Rebecca." he said, looking up at Leo. Marcus gets up and walks over to the desk. He looks over Carlos's shoulder at the screen, "I'll go check out the address." Craig grabs Leo's keys off the desk, "Let's go," he says as they walked out the door.

Jerry approaches Sam as he packed their supply bag, "Sam, we need new rides. I can go fine some!" he said quietly. Sam nods in agreement with Jerry as Carlos continues to search the police files. Leo looks out the window watching his friends as they drove off. Leo shows no emotion, even though he knew that they are risking their lives to help him. Leo stood at the window for a while looking out into the darkness of the night.

He shakes his head, "Leanna was just going to the store, only if I had told her not to go, she would be here with me," he said as he sits on the edge of the table. Crossing his arms, he looks over at Sam and Carlos, "Thank you for helping me."

Surprised by Leo's words, Sam and Carlos look at him. Carlos shakes his empty cup at Leo, "We're going to find him." Leo grabs the cup from Carlos and fills it with ice and rum. Carlos looks back at the monitor, "Hey there is a file here for a guy name Mark who died in a bar fight." Sam pulls the laptop closer to him as Leo leans over Sam's shoulder. Leo didn't recognize the man's name, but he remembered the face. Leo leans closer to the monitor, "Sam that's the guy that pushed me that night at the bar," he said as recognition set in. He hands Carlos his drink and takes the laptop off the desk. He walks over to the bed and sits on the edge of the bed. "Yes, that's him," Leo says as he continues to scroll through the pages of the report. He noticed that the report says Mark has a brother named Luke, who served time for murder. Leo looks over at Carlos, "Can you find all the flights in and out of New York in the last three months matching Luke's description?" he asks. Carlos walks over to

Leo, "That's child's play. I'll pull Luke's file while I'm at it to see if there is anything else we need to know about this guy."

As Carlo, Sam, and Leo search through the files, Marcus and Craig find Rebecca's Street. Pulling up to Rebecca's address, Craig and Marcus drove slowly down the street. Craig parks the car a few houses down, then the two men walked back to check out Rebecca's house.

Craig and Marcus went around to the back of the house to check if anyone was home. With no one home, they forced their way into the house to check out the inside. Craig took out his cell phone and took some photos of the family photographs that were on the wall. While Marcus moves to the back of the house checking the bedroom. He yells for Craig to come to the master room, "Check this out," he says, pointing to the nightstand. Craig looks at the documents sprawled in front of him. On the nightstand, there were photos of Leanna and her medical records. Craig quickly scans all the information into his phone and then the two men left Rebecca's house and headed back to their motel.

Chapter Four

Jerry drove through the mall parking lot looking at the cars.

He decides that their get-a-way cars needed to be unmarked and

untraceable. He drove for another twenty minutes and pulls into a

night club. He begins to walk inside of the club when he was spotted

by their security. The guard told Jerry to follow him to the upstairs

room. The guard opens the door and a man dressed in all red turns

and looked at Jerry, "Look at this fucking loser... my baby brother...

I thought you were dead?" he said with a smirk.

Jerry slowly walks into the room, "Sorry to disappoint you, I

walk among the living Albert." Albert gets in Jerry's face and

screams, "Everyone, out, now!" All the dancers rush out of the room.

Albert points at Jerry's chest, "No one calls me Albert anymore. I go

by Al now." Jerry puts his hands up and takes a few steps backwards,

"I can see you're the man now," he said with respect. Albert walks

over to his desk, "Why are you here? We agreed not to meet at my

place of business."

Jerry walks over to the desk and sits down on the chair. He

leans forward and takes some candy off the desk, "Leo's girl Leanna was murdered, and we need some rides… unmarked cars…. With all the fixings to get the job done." Albert shakes his head saying, "The last time I helped you I lost over 100,000 dollars," as he pours some wine into two red crystal wine glasses. He walks over to Jerry and hands him a wine glass. Jerry takes the glass and looks at Albert, "Leo would do it for you."

Albert takes a sip of the wine then he raised his glass to Jerry. Albert told Jerry to show up at the shop at 10 pm tomorrow night. Jerry drinks the wine and puts down his glass on the desk. He walks to the door and stops as he looks straight ahead, he mumbles, "How is mom?"

Albert looks up at Jerry, "Still praying for the prodigal son to return home."

Jerry walks out the room taking the stairs and disappearing into the night. Albert sits in his golden chair. He turns and looks out into the crowded street.

Twenty minute later Jerry shows up at the motel with dinner a bag full of greasy burgers. He kicks the door, "Honey, I'm home." Sam opens the door for Jerry. Carlos jumps up and reaches for the food, he then throws Leo a burger. As the friends sat and eat, Sam fills Jerry in on the new information. Marcus and Craig walk into the room and Carlos hands them their dinner. Craig walks over to the laptop and uploads the images scouted from Rebecca's house off his phone to the laptop. Craig joins Leo on the couch. Leo studies the images then lean back in his seat, "This is our guy, this is Luke, I will never forget his face, and I want his head."

Sam nobs with approval, he turns to Leo and tells him "By tomorrow night, you will have his head." Craig tells the team that Rebecca was Leanna's nurse at the hospital and that Luke has been watching the house for months with the help of Rebecca's boyfriend Michael who is Luke's older cousin. Marcus eats his burger as he nods in agreement. Leo gets up from the couch and looks at the image of Leanna on his phone's home screen, "Now that we know who killed Leanna and our son, I want them to pay."

Jerry glances at Leo, "Get some rest, we've got an early start and a long day ahead of us." he says looking around at the group. Suddenly, the computer beeps and Carlos hurries over to the desk, "Rebecca's credit card was used 20 miles away at a motel. I'll tap in their cameras to see who used the credit card," he said as reviewed the screen. Carlos took his computer to his room and the rest of the team when to their rooms. Sam sits on the couch while Leo takes a shower. Sam looks at the files as they replay on the television monitor, he walks over and turns it off.

In the shower Leo laid his head against the wall while the water runs down his back. He thinks about how Leanna would rub his back. He remembers how he would kiss her gently and make love to her in the shower. Just then, Sam knocks on the door, "Hey man, save me some hot water." Leo turns off the water, grabs a towel and walks out of the bathroom mad. "Go shower in your own fucking room," he says angrily at Sam. Sam watches him walk off, his eyebrow raising in confusion as he takes off his shirt and walks into the bathroom. He mumbles to himself "somebody has to babysit your crazy ass."

After a long night the team got some rest. In the morning they went back to Leo's room to go over the plan. Leo made the decision to have Craig and Jerry follow Rebecca. Craig and Jerry quickly agreed to their new assignments, and they rushed over to the hospital. Craig walks in the hospital and saw that Rebecca was there. It was time to put the plan into action. He rushes over to Rebecca, begging for help as Jerry laid in the car faking sick. Rebecca runs out to the car to attend to the patient as Craig nervously sits and acts as his overbearing lover.

Once Rebecca's shift ended, Jerry and Craig got in their car and followed Rebecca. She made several stops throughout the night. Rebecca's last stops was at a restaurant where she picked up dinner, then she went to the abandoned house. Jerry and Craig parked their car a few houses down. As they sat outside, they watched the abandoned house to see if Luke was there.

Sam and Leo arrived late at Albert's shop to pick up their new cars. Albert anxiously awaits by the front door smoking his cigarette. As Leo and Sam approached, Albert put out his cigarette, "When the lion calls, we answer. For the bite of the lion is deadly, especially a mad lion." He tosses Leo the keys and points to the trailer at the end of the building, then he walks off. Leo and Sam walk over to the trailer and Sam unlocks the door, swinging it open, he peers into the trailer, smiling with approval of the new cars. Craig calls Leo, as they stake out the abandoned home, keeping a close watch on Luke. He tells Leo that the location is perfect and that they should make their move tonight. Leo quickly agrees. In the darkness of the night Leo, Sam, Carlos, and Marcus showed up to the abandoned house with their gear on and their guns drawn. Leo gives the signal as Craig, and Jerry creeps slowly to the back of the house. Marcus and Carlos anxiously wait in their cars as they watch the streets. Leo walks over to the side door and waits, while Sam lays in the overgrown grass with his sniper gun covering the front door.

Craig throws a homemade gas bomb into the kitchen window scaring Rebecca. Rebecca screams and runs out the kitchen through the side door. At that moment, Leo grabs her, covering her mouth as Craig and Jerry enter the home through the kitchen door, clearing the rooms as they make their way through the house. Leo slowly walks in through the side door that led to the dining room, using Rebecca as a shield.

Luke was hiding just behind the door, and he rushes toward Leo as he walked into the dining room, knocking Rebecca to the floor with a loud thud. Leo grabs Luke by the throat and slams him to the floor, then he picks him up and throws him into the wall, the drywall giving way with strain of the fight. As Luke crashed to the floor, he pulls out his knife and stabs Leo in his thigh and manages to break loose from Leo's grip.

Jerry sees movement in the bathroom. He tap's Craig on his shoulder signaling the movement in the bathroom. They make their way down the dark hallway. At the same time, Rebecca gets up off the floor and runs down the hallway, coming face to face with Craig and Jerry. Startled at seeing the men, geared up and in the house, she screams for help. Michael opens the bathroom door and opens fire on Craig and Jerry, accidentally killing Rebecca. Michael sees Rebecca laying on the floor, he positions himself as he tries to pull her into the bathroom. He looks up and sees Craig and Jerry standing over him he begs for his life as they execute him.

Luke tries to run out the living room, Leo throws a chair at Luke hitting his legs slowing him down. He grabs Luke as they fought making their way to the front of the house knocking over everything in their path. Luke reaches and open the front door as Leo rushes him. Sam sees movement toward the front of the house, he slowly approaches the door. Leo grabs Luke, slamming him to the floor. He quickly gets back up on his feet, throwing a lamp at Leo as he jumps backwards through the window shooting into the house, forcing Leo to run into the other room.

Luke ran down the abandon street with Marcus and Carlos in pursuit in their cars. Luke opens fire at Marcus, causing him to hit the light pole. Luke continued running and jumping over the gate and escaping through the streets. Marcus and Carlos jump out of their cars, chasing after Luke on foot as they call for back up. Leo and Sam got into their car and tried to cut Luke off at the end of the street, but he never came out. Luke knew the area very well and he was able to escape his fate that night.

Jerry and Craig searched the house. They came across Luke's laptop, money, Rebecca, and Michael's passports, and two airline tickets to Puerto Rico. Jerry grabs the laptop and the money as Craig takes the passports and airline ticket. Jerry sets the timer on the gas stove as they exit the house. Jerry sets off a chain reaction of several explosions, destroying the abandoned house and everything in it. All the abandoned homes in the area went up in flames as the men searched the streets hunting Luke. They drove for hours but Luke was nowhere in sight. Leo orders the team to go back to the motel.

Chapter Five

Retreating to their motel Sam, Jerry, Marcus, Carlos, and Craig begins to unpack their cars. Leo was extremely upset that Luke got away, flipping over the trash can in his frustration. Craig drops his bags, he rushes over to Leo and pushes him in the chest, "Let it out, hit me." Leo refuses to hit him, he walks off. Jerry walked up to Craig he uses his shoulder to shove Craig out of his way as he walked through the door.

Exhausted, the team went to Leo's motel room and crumpled to the floor for the night. Leo sat alone in the back of his work truck for an hour. He looks at the moon and started to think about Leanna's moon shaped birth mark on her neck. He remembers how she would laugh when he kissed her birth mark. He gets up and hops out of the truck bed and went back to the room. Inside, he looks around, then he looks at Sam, "I can smell Leanna." He said with a concern voice.

Carlos looks over at the desk he noticed that his laptop and all of Leanna's files was missing. He pulls out his backup laptop from his bag and begins to track his computer. That night as the team slept on the floor, Carlos stays up all night tracking his computer he yells at the team, "Wakeup, wakeup! We are going to Puerto Rico." He leans in to take a closer look at the location, "We might not make it back." he said while eyeing the location. Craig sits up yawning as he stretches, "Why?" he asked. Carlos shows him the laptop screen, "The computer is at Troy's."

The name Troy sends a cold chill down Leo's back, this was a name that Leo's team knew very well. Leo gets up from the couch, he glances at Carlos, "Let go get it," he said in a serious tone. He starts to pack his bags. Everyone follows suit and the team packs in a hurry. They made their way to the airport, traveling as strangers on vacation. At the airport Marcus made a few calls and he was able to rent a van and a villa for the week. Upon hearing this news, Sam looks at Leo as he remembers their last encounter with the Troy, "We might not make it a week. We are marching towards our death."

Marcus went to the car rental desk to rent the van and was greeted by a friendly clerk, "Hi, how may I help you?" Marcus hands her his driver's license, "I'm here to pick up a van I rented." She takes his fake identification, "The villa has already arranged your transportation. you're your driver should be pulling up shortly," she said with a smile, giving Marcus back his fake identification. He walks back over to his team and waited for their ride. The van pulled into the car rental areas and team hops in the van.

They drove for an hour before reaching the gated villa. The van turned into the long winding driveway of the villa. The groundskeeper greets the team and walks them to the door. There, two maids approach the team with ice-cold tropical drinks. Leo wasted no time rubbing his palms together. He walks to the middle of the room meeting the maid and getting his drink. In celebration mode, Jerry cheers to the start of their trip and the team drunk their welcome drinks, quietly anticipating what was to come.

Suddenly, there was a loud clapping coming from the distance. The team was on guard as Troy entered the room, clapping his hands. The sound of his hands clapping together echoes through the room like thunder. He strolls in, "This is too easy, just like that you walk into the silverback's nest," he said, coming to a stop in the center of the room.

Thinking the worst, Craig looks down at his drinks. Troy laughs at him, "Your drinks are safe. Poisoning you is for the weak hearted, and that's not my style." Sam moves behind the couch as Troy signals his security guards to search them.

Troy gazed at Sam "I see you're still a watch dog. Good boy, down Sam, down boy." He walks over to the table making fun of Sam. Troy pulls out the chair and sat down. He challenges Leo to arm wrestle him. Leo sits and positions himself, knowing that he was no match for his big brother. Troy was ten times stronger than Leo. His size and strength made him a feared man. His friends and enemies alike called him 'The Silverback'. The brothers had different mothers and Troy always made sure to remind Leo of this. He saw Leo as weak and throughout their childhood, he made it his mission to make Leo into the man their father was. Troy smiles at Leo, taunting him. Leo remembers the last time his brother challenged him, the challenge that almost cost Leo his life.

Suddenly, Leo smelled Leanna's perfume and then he heard her footsteps in a distance. He looks at his brother wondering what he has done. The team looks down the hallway as a woman approaches out of the darkness of the hallway. Leo gets up, he walks towards the mysterious woman meeting her in the middle of the room, "Leanna," he gasped, falling to his knees. The women in all white emerged from the darkness with fire in her eyes. She pulls out her gun and places it to his brow, "Murderer, you killed my sister."

Troy notices the pain in Leo's eyes, the same pain his mother had when their dad died. He points at the mystery woman "Anna, you promised me that you would play nice with our guests." Anna cocked the gun, pressing it into Leo's brow.

Sam, Marcus, Carlos, Craig, and Jerry showed no fear as they approach the Anna. Troy sees that Leo's team was willing to die for him. Leo, put his hand up, he begs Anna, "Kill me, I am already dead." Troy yells for the maid to bring more drinks. The maid approaches. Anna looks at the maid, as she smirked. She leaned in and whispers in Leo's ear, "Dying is easy, living is hard. You, Leo, will live forever." She puts her gun away and orders Mia, her personal maid, to bring drinks to her room. Leo's team was speechless as Anna walks down the long hallway disappearing in the darkness. Jerry walks to the end of the hallway and watches Anna as she walks out of his sight, "That's Leanna's sister…?" he asks in disbelief. Troy helps Leo up onto his feet as Leo struggles to understand what was happening.

Troy's sees the confusion on Leo's face, "Brother sit with me and let me explain."
Leo walks over to the chair, he sat in silence, expressionless as Troy continues to talk, "When I heard about Leanna's death, I came to

visit you. Then I decided to stay in the shadows close enough to keep an eye on things. The night you and your team went after Luke, I saw Anna breaking in your motel room and stealing Carlos's laptop. When she tried to exit the room, I grabbed her."

Troy ensures Leo and his team that the past should stay in the past, "Let's not look back on the past, the future starts now," he said sincerely. With the team all caught up, Leo requests to meet with Anna alone. Troy agrees to his request and tells his most trusted guard Sean to escort Leo to Anna's room. Sean and Leo walked down the long hallway in silence. Sean stops in front of a door, he looks at Leo, "I know your brother can be a handful, just know that he got your back," Sean says as he knocks on the room door.

Mia, Anna's personal maid, opens the door. She smiled at Leo as she rushes out of the room. In the next moment, Anna walks out of the bathroom, she sees Leo and Sean standing by the door. She shows Sean her middle finger and he smirked as he turns and walks back down the long hallway. She looks at Leo with hate, "You have some fucking nerve…. because of you my sister is dead," she said angrily. Leo looks at Anna he sees the close resemblance of his Leanna. Anna notices the way he looks at her, she sighs, "I'm not your precious Leanna, she was weak. I am nothing like her… your

Leanna was mommy and daddy's precious, perfect little girl," she said as she sauntered over and sat on the bed. Leo closes the door and walks slowly into the room, "You're nothing like Leanna. She was kind, gentle, perfect, and I will find the man that took her from me," he declared, leaning on the wall. Anna could see that Leo was still in love with her sister, yet she refuses to let him forget that he was the cause of her death. The intercom goes off in the room. Troy requests their immediate presence in the lounge.

Chapter Six

The team sits in the lounge waiting for the arrival of Troy. Sean approaches Leo and asks him to follow. Sam and Craig got up, but Leo signals for them to stand down. Leo follows Sean out of the room as the team waits in the lounge. Sean leads Leo into a room with an amazing view. Troy sits comfortably by the pool, he looks out at the ocean view, talking to himself, "Who puts a pool by the ocean, what the hell was I thinking?"

Leo approaches him, Troy acknowledges Leo's presence, and the two brothers talk among themselves keeping their distance. Troy informs Leo that he got word that Luke is on the island. Leo walks over to Troy, "Where is he?" he asks. Troy sighs at Leo, "I don't know, plus you're not doing this on your own." Leo leans over the wall as he looks at the ocean view from the balcony, "I'm not alone, I have my team."

Troy joins him on the balcony, he looks at him "Leo, your team is made up of a bunch of old rundown ex-marine drunks. This is not a joke, Luke has you out numbered here. We do this together;

dad would want that." Leo crosses his arm, "I can't forgive, and I can't forget," he says in defiance. Troy nods in agreement. He looks out at the still water, "I'm not asking you too. This will be our only chance to get Luke, it must be perfect." Troy turns and looks at Leo. He places the palm of his hand on Leo's chest, "Brother, we do this together there is no other way."

Leo and Troy walk back into the lounge together and the room gets quiet. Sam, Marcus, Jerry, and Craig stood up. Anna looks at the brothers, questioning their strange relationship. Sam smiled, knowing that the duo is more deadly together. He was proud to see the brothers had set aside their differences and were working together. Leo begins to speak to the team, and he informs everyone that Luke was on the island and in hiding. Troy walks over to Leo, he looks at their team and says, "Enjoy the night, training starts tomorrow."

As the team exits the lounge Troy signals for Anna, and she approaches Troy hands her a letter, "I need you and Leo to take this letter to big Jon's restaurant." Snatching the letter from Troy's hand, "Damn, why? Send Leo, Mia is waiting for me," she said in exasperation. Troy raises an eyebrow. Anna frowns and rolls her eyes at Leo, "I guess I'm stuck babysitting you! Let's make this quick," Anna demand, storming off. Leo shakes his head and follows behind her.

Frustrated, Anna starts the truck and pulls out of the long curvy driveway. The car ride to Big Jon's place took forever as Leo and Anna sit quietly. The silence started to get to Leo, he glanced at Anna, "Who is big Jon?" She sighs, "I was told that Big Jon is the man that can make things happen. Whatever you need, big Jon will get it. Due to this big Jon is well-known and respected on the island so don't do anything stupid," she shot back with a warning glance. With a name like Big Jon, there is no telling what will happen; Leo sends his location to his team. Carlos patiently watches his location on his computer, ready and waiting.

Troy urges his security guard Sean to bring Sam, Jerry, Marcus, Jerry, and Craig to his office immediately. When the team arrives to the office, Troy met them at the door, "Come in, we need to talk."

Sean, his personal guard tries to enter the office after them, Troy's stopped him, "No, just these five," he closes the door and Sean waits right outside the door. Troy walks over to his desk and sat in his golden chair. He points at the couch and the team sits. Troy looks at them, "You know that my relationship with Leo is a confusing one with many conflicts. But I love my brother, and he loves you all." The team nods with agreement, Troy sits back in his chair, and puts his hand on his chin, "Leo is over his head. You boys are way past your prime and so am I. We need to work together to get the job done."

Craig crosses his arms, "Unlike you, we have always been there for Leo." Troy nods with agreement. After a few hours of talking the team agrees to put aside their differences as they work together. Troy explains to the team what they will be up against going face to face with Luke. Meanwhile, Leo and Anna pull up to Big Jon's restaurant. The rundown building was crowded with people eating, drinking, and having a good time. They walk up to the main door and was told to wait there. Out of nowhere, an old frail man walks up to the door and greets them as he struggles to open the door. He asks them, "Are you here for the party?" Leo opens the door for the old man, "No, we're waiting to see Big Jon we have a letter for him."

The old man takes a closer look at Leo face, "A letter… from who?" Anna shows the old man the envelope with the silverback's stamp. The old man looks at the envelope, "Come, come, I'll take you to Big Jon." They follow the old man inside the restaurant and through an oversized brass door. The old man uses his key to unlock a mysterious looking door. "Come in, come in," the old man says as he sits on the floor. Anna stands by the door with her arms crossed as she looks around the room.

Leo joins the old man on the floor. He looks around the room, "Where is Big Jon?"
The old man studies Leo's face, "You have your fathers face... he was a good man. Your father, he used to call me Big Jon, because he could not remember my real name and the name Big Jon just stuck." Leo takes a closer look at the man as he tries to remember his face.

Anna walks over to big Jon, "Here!" She hands him the letter, and he begin to read in silence.
After a while, he looks up at Leo, "Tell the silverback Big Jon says yes." He glances over at Anna, "The fire in your eyes will not burn for long." Anna walks out and slams the door behind her. Leo sits with the old man for a while, and they begin to talk about Leo's father.

Anna sits alone outside the restaurant as she waits for Leo. She sees two little girls playing in the sand and she remembers playing with her sister when they were younger. She smiles as the waitress approaches her table, "You need something, Hun?"

Anna bites her lips, as she studies the waitress's hips. She puts her feet up on the table, "What I need is not on the menu." The waitress leans closer to Anna, "Honey, whatever you want we can get it for you." Anna smiles at the waitress, "I could use a drink," she says. The waitress gives her the two beers that were on her tray.

Big Jon walks Leo over to Anna, "I'll leave you two here, see you soon." Big Jon walks to his car, he stops and look back at Leo, he sighs as he drives off. Anna and Leo watch the two little girls playing in the sand. Leo takes the beer off the table and takes a drink, "I know you miss your sister, I do too." Anna takes a drink, "You really do love her! Leo, I forgive you. I just hope my sister forgives me too."

Leo pulls the chair out and sits by Anna, "She does, she really loved you. Leanna was always talking about your adventures and how close you two used to be." Leo glances at Anna, "What happened between you two? You were so close," he inquired gently. Anna takes her feet off the table and sits back in her chair, "I left home because our dad didn't want Leanna to catch my disease. Having one gay daughter was enough," she said as she gazed at the ocean, she takes a sip of her beer. Leo orders some more drink and the two sat silently for hours.

Before long, the night comes to an end. As the restaurant closes, the two made their way to the truck. Upon arriving at the villa, Leo could tell that Anna was drunk. As she stumbles to get out of the truck, he helps her. He quickly catches her from falling, "I got you." Mia was waiting for Anna at the door, she runs to meet Leo as she sees him carrying Anna. Mia was worried, "What happened to her?" yelling at him.

Leo lifts Anna in his arms, "She's okay, she just drunk and needs to sleep it off. Get the door," he said signaling with his chin. Mia runs to open and close the door for Leo. He lays Anna down onto the bed. Seeing Anna, sleeping he remembers when Leanna would lay in is arms. Anna opens her eyes, smiling at Leo as she gets up, she reaches for Mia, she pulls her over to the bed kissing her. Leo quickly looks away. He leaves Anna's room and goes upstairs to meet with Troy.

He knocks on Troy's office door and there was no answer, so he lets himself into Troy's office. "Troy?" Leo asks into the darkness. Troy sits alone in the dark room looking out at the moon, "Over here," he called out, "a full moon is coming." Leo walks over to Troy, "Big Jon told me about dad." Troy turns in his chair as he rocks it, back and forth, "Good, now you know. What was Big Jon's answer?"

Leo crossed his arms "Big Jon's answer is yes, but what was the question?" Troy gets up as he ignores Leo's query, "Good night, Leo. We got a long day ahead of us." Troy walks out of the office and went to his room across the hall. Leo looks up at the moon. He walks over to the desk, studying the moon. As he sits in Troy's chair, he sees a bracelet on the desk. Leo picks up the bracelet, examining the image of a silverback on the bracelet. The bracelet was an exact match to the one that Carlos gave him. He wonders, "Why would Carlos give Troy a bracelet?"

Leo decides to remove his bracelet from his wrist. The bracelet tightens around his wrist and would not release. He tried a few times, but he could not unlock the bracelet.

Chapter Seven

Frustrated about the bracelet, Leo went to his room and lays in bed. He closes his eyes as he thinks of his beloved Leanna. He hears Anna and Mia making love in the next room. He bangs on the wall, yelling "Shut up!" In the morning three SUVs arrive to pick up the team. Without any questions, they go with Troy. They drove for Thirty minutes before pulling up to a large ranch. There, Big Jon was waiting for their arrival. He signals them where to park. Once everyone unloads from the vehicles, Big Jon embraces Troy and Leo, as he greets everyone by their name and specialty.

Big Jon was filled with excitement, "Welcome to camp, today you train," The team looks over at the different stations, and began to make their way to their assigned stations. Anna reaches for a sword. She looks at Leo as she shows off her skill. Carlos went for the technology while Sam embraced and kisses the sniper guns. Jerry hugs the demolition supplies, kissing them as Craig walks around him, he yells "Get a room!" He goes over to the heavy machine guns, "Oh yes! Talk to daddy."

Marcus shakes his head at Craig, "what a sick little man" as he walks over to check out the cars that were parked on the green grass. He opens the car door "oh, yes open up for daddy." He sits inside the truck, and takes a deep breath "brand new, just the way daddy likes it." Leo stands by the table as he observes the different types of knives. Big Jon nods with approval, "Just like your dad," he gives Leo an axe.

The team train throughout the day and late into the night. Big Jon approves of their work as he watches the team from the barn. An old bell hangs in the rafters just about Big Jon's head. He reaches up with a gnarled hand and rings the bell, "Time to eat!" he croons. Soon the team is heading back to the barn house. Inside there was a large table filled with an abundance of food for the team to eat. As everyone gathers to eat, Big Jon told his old war story about his friends and how their dad saved his life.

Anna was able to see the side of Leo that Leanna fell in love with. Troy was able to be a brother to Leo that night. Leo's team sees him laughing again for the first time since Leanna's death. Big Jon gives Leo a cup of tea, "Drink up, you'll sleep better tonight." Thanking the old man, Leo drinks the tea. Everyone had full bellies and soon it was time for dinner to come to an end. Big Jon told them their assigned rooms and the team bid each other good night as they went their separate ways.

Upon entering their rooms, the team saw their equipment, supplies and clothing on their bed. Leo went up to his room and sees an axe on the bed. He picks up the axe and felt the blades. Testing the weight, he put the gears on the nightstand. He enters the bathroom where he takes a long hot shower. While Leo lets the hot water run down his body, Anna knocks on his room door. Hearing no answer, she lets herself in and sits on the bed waiting for him. She hears the water as he turns it off. With lust in her eye, Anna watches him in the mirror as he wraps the towel around his waist. Leo walks into the bedroom and sees Anna sitting on his bed with her legs open.

He was shocked and did not utter a word, he stood still with a confused look on his face. She gets up and slowly walks over to him. Leo remains still and speechless not knowing what Anna was about to do. Anna stands on her tippy toes, she leans in and kisses him. He gently pushes her back. She gets in closer, kissing him again. Leo closes his eyes, Anna's lips felt like Leanna's lips. He could smell Leanna's perfume and he could feel her warmth.

Leo felt as if he was kissing Leanna, embracing her as he lifts her closer to him. Anna wraps her legs around his waist. Leo gets lost in the moment as he lays Anna onto the bed. He looks into Anna's green eyes and pulls back, realizing that it was Anna, "I can't, you're not Leanna," he said turning away.

Anna climbs on top of him and undoes her curly hair. Leo could only see his beloved Leanna in the moon light. He couldn't resist Anna anymore and that night Leo made love to Anna. Throughout the night Leo held her and calls her Leanna. Anna embraces Leo that night just as Leanna would have, as the full moon shines on their wet skin.

The next morning Anna woke up and snuck back to her room. She stares at the clock as she lays in her bed, thinking about what she did. Later that day Leo woke up, he laid in the bed staring at the sky light unable to tell if it was a dream or was it real. He remembers that his beloved Leanna was gone but he shows no emotions. He gets up and sit at the edge of the bed with a blank look on his face. Big Jon knocks at the door, "Wake up, it's time to go," he bellows. Leo dresses quickly and opens the door. Big Jon walks into the room. He tells Big Jon about the strange dream he had about Leanna. Big Jon knew the truth, but he assures Leo that it was a dream and that dreams are the way we communicate with the ones we've lost. He knew Leo needed to feel Leanna's warmth one more time.

Troy rushes into the room, "I got news that Luke's making his move tonight, my team is already in place." With that announcement, everyone springs into action. Leo puts on his shirt and rushes out the door. Big Jon and Carlos walks to the end of the driveway as the team pulls off. Big Jon wishes them the best. Carlos heads back to the security room where he signs into his computers and gets ready to work. On their way to the party, Troy fills Leo in on Luke's hide out and the reason he will leave his hide out. The only thing Leo could think about was the night Luke took Leanna away from him. He could hear her screaming as Luke carved his name in her growing belly. Troy notices the change on Leo's face. He taps Leo on his shoulder, "Welcome back Lion." The men gear up for war.

Carlos checks in on the team and their position as he informs them that Luke was staying with his cousin's and that the compound has a total of twenty guards, plus the local gang that acts as look out on the roads. Troy was able to get two of his men inside the walls of the compound. They would be guarding Luke as he makes this appearance at his uncle's birthday party.

The team will have only one chance to pull this off. They will be going up against Luke's guards, friends, family, and the street gang. With everyone in place, one of Troy's spy's left the gate unlocked, giving the team access to the party. Anna dresses for the occasion as a dancer for the guest. Leo and Troy wait patiently in the car. Leo looks over and sees the bracelet on Troy's arm. While Sam, Jerry and Craig work the party as waiters, Marcus works in the kitchen which is the known entrance route for Luke.

Carlos gets news of Luke's arrival time. He informs the team as they listen in on their earpieces. Three hours later and Luke was nowhere to be seen. Chef Marcus was asked to greet the guests and work the room. Craig went to cover the kitchen; he starts to clean the grill as he moves closer to the door. Marcus works the room, mingling with the guests and entertaining the family. Hastily, Luke's team of guards walk in and asks everyone to leave the kitchen. Craig quickly hides in the closet as Luke enters the kitchen, surrounded by his ten personal guards.

Troy's spy drops his keys to signal the arrival of Luke. Craig hears the keys and sends a text notification to Carlos. Carlos then informs Jerry and Sam in their earpiece that Luke is in the building. On schedule, Anna made her way up to the security room where she dances and flirts with the guards, "We can have our own party here," she says as she grinds seductively. The men watch her as she dances for them. Giving Carlos enough time to tap in the security cameras. Carlos now has full control of all the cameras in the compound and he could see the location of the team.

Big Jon intensely looks on the computer monitor. He watches Luke's movement while Carlos tells Jerry to go to the security room to help Anna. Luke enters the party, hugging his family as he walks through the crowd. His family and guests praise him. His uncle sits at the head of the long black table.

Luke walks over to greet his uncle as the old man gets up and hugs his nephew, "My boy, so glad you made it" he smiled as he slowly sits back down into his chair. Luke reaches into his pocket and pulls out a blue box, he hands the box to his uncle, "Happy birthday uncle." The old man opens the box and reaches out to Luke, kisses his cheeks as he thanks him for his gift. In the box there was a beautiful heirloom, a blue diamond ring.

The old man put on the ring that Luke gifted, he boldly and proudly shows the crowd. As they cheer with admiration, he tells the guest "Sit and eat with me," he gestures to the servants to serve his guests. Luke sits at the table with his uncle. The uncle signals for Sam to bring them wine. Sam pours their wine, as Luke and his uncle talk about the good food that's on the menu. Sam stays close to Luke as dancers enter the room, dancing and entertaining the men and their guests.

Jerry made it to the security room with drinks for the security guards. Looking at the champagne bottles, the guards let him in and that's when Anna pulls out her gun. She taps one of the guards on his head "You know what this is, sit." Jerry and Anna successfully took over the control room. Jerry looks at Anna as she begins to tie up the men. He aims for their heads and assassinate all three of the security guards. Ann looks at him in disbelief and Jerry rushes out the room, "I'm sorry," he says as he locks Anna in the control room. She screams for him to let her out, as he stands by the door shaking his head, "You're safer here." He runs back down the hall and went back downstairs to the party.

Carlos speaks to Anna, telling her that he needs her to calm down and to turn off the lights in the main dining area. Cursing Jerry, she looks for the light switch. While Leo and Troy wait at the back door for the room to go dark, Marcus continues to work the room, entertaining the guests as he made his way over to Luke's table. Jerry and Craig walk in with their tray as Sam stays close to the side door. Suddenly, the room went dark, this signal Leo and Troy to run over to the door. With their mask on, Sam quickly opens the door, letting them in.

Chapter Eight

Big Jon and Carlos held their breath as the lights came back on. Anna rushes over to the computer, she sat and watches the monitor. As she intensely watches their next move. Sam, Craig, Jerry, Marcus, Troy, and Leo pull their guns, and on que they assassinate all of Luke's personal security guards. The room went quiet as the guards lay lifeless on the floor. As realization began to set in, the guests started to scream. Troy yells, "Shut up!" His voice shook the room, and everyone stood in silence. Luke looks on in disbelief at the sight of all the dead guards.

Leo pulls off his mask and Luke's soul left his body at the sight of Leo's face. Luke jumps up and reaches for his gun, but Leo quickly pulls out his knife and cuts off four of Luke's fingers. Luke drops his gun on the black table as he screams in pain. Leo looks at him with a scowl. Luke looks up at Leo, as he wipes his knife on the uncle's white shirt sleeves. Leo never brakes eye contact with Luke as he cleans his blade. Luke smirks at Leo, "She was tight, the best I ever had." he said, holding Leo's gaze wearing a sick, twisted grin. Leo stares into Luke's eyes until he could see his own reflection.

Leo remains silent as he pulls his axe from his gear. With one swing of the axe, he chops Luke's uncle's ring from his finger. The old man falls to the floor, doubled over in pain. Luke was shocked as he looks down at his uncle. Leo takes Luke's gun and shoots the old man in his brow. Luke starts to beg Leo to stop, but for him there is no mercy. Leo looks around the room, at the frighten and scared faces. He sees Luke's aunt trying to hide in the back of the room. He calmly throws his knife killing Luke's aunt. Then he signals Craig, Sam, Jerry, Marcus, and Troy to take care of the rest of the guests as the family watches in shock. The family begs for their lives. The team mercilessly assassinate all the guests of the family as Luke watches and begs Leo to let his family go.

Leo remains silent and did not utter a word. Troy looks over at the family, "Your free to go." The family rushes to the door, and the team opens fire, killing everyone at the party. Luke sits in shock as his fingers bleed. The sounds of screaming, and the gun fire echoes through the street, drawing the gang members to the compound. As the gangs begin to move in, they creep through the main door of the home. Sam, Jerry, Craig, Troy, and Marcus change the clips in their guns. Troy orders his two guards to go to the back of the compound, covering the back of the house. Leo looks at his team, "tonight, we will be the only ones who will walk out of here alive," he said in a stern voice. The team fueled with rage and vengeance as they meet the gang members at the front doors. Their wrath grow as they all open fire on the gang members. Excited, Troy joins in on the massacre. The walls, floors, and pool turn red with blood as the last gang member falls to the floor. Leo took his axe in his hand and with one chop Luke's head fell to the floor. Leo picks up his prize in his hand as he screams out with rage.

Jerry rushes back to the security room to get Anna. As he opens the door, she embraces him. Slowly they made their way downstairs, Anna slips on the blood covered stairs, luckily Jerry catches her. Anna stood in shock, as she watches Leo with Luke's head in hand, screaming in carnal rage, he was covered in blood, as the rest of the team celebrates their win. At that moment Anna saw that Leo was not the man she thought he was. Now she understands why he was called the mad lion, as he stands surrounded by carnage, covered in Luke's blood. Leo got what he came for. Excited with the success of the hunt, he throws Luke's head in the fireplace and watches it as it burns. Anna's watches Leo with fear as her blood runs cold.

Big Jon and Carlos hug each other as they celebrate the success of the team. Big Jon rushes to the door, ordering the maids to get dinner for the king. The team exits the bloody home, and Jerry throws several of his homemade explosion in the house. The team stands outside as they watch the flames rise. They got in their cars and headed back to Big Jon's farm. During the ride back, Leo remains quiet as the team celebrates their success.

As they pull up to the camp, Big Jon greeted them. Leo shows no emotions as he hastily went to his room. He looks at himself in the mirror, covered in Luke's blood. He takes of his clothing and throws them in the hallway. He walks into the shower standing under the hot water, letting the blood wash off his face, down his body, and into the drain. He closes his eyes, but Leanna was not there. Leo cries, letting the tears flow freely. Now he understands that his beloved Leanna was now gone forever.

Big Jon walks down the hallway and sees Leo soil clothing on the floor. He picks up the clothing and listens at the door, he hears Leo crying, "I know, I know it still hurts." Big Jon heads back to the party. As he walks through the kitchen, he looks over at Anna as she dances with Mia. Carlos and Troy watch the ladies, cheering them on and throwing money at them.

Craig, Marcus, Jerry, and Sam sit by the fire pit as Big Jon and the maids burn their clothing. Leo walks to the balcony of his room, he stood there looking out into the night. He watches his team as they celebrate the lion's successful hunt. He went down and joined them. A few hours later Carlos looks at the time and hugs his friend goodbye. It was time for him head back home to this family in Mexico. Leo walks Carlos to the car thanking him for coming as he reaches in his pocket. He gives Carlos the ring he took from Luke's uncle, "I'm sorry you miss out on the action." Carlos smiles and puts the ring on his finger as the men part ways. The driver starts making the journey toward the airport and Carlos looks out the window at Leo.

With the rising of the sun, it was time for Anna to go home. She gets up and begins to pack her bags. Mia gets up from their bed and wrap the sheer white sheet around her body as she begs to go with her. Anna kisses Mia goodbye, Mia fell to the floor crying as Anna left the room. Closing the door behind her, Anna rests her head at the door. She rushes to Troy's office, there Troy was looking at some papers. When she burst through the door, she thanks him for everything.

Remembering Mia, she asks Troy's permission to take Mia with her to Japan. Troy reaches in his desk draw and gave Anna a brown envelope. Anna opens the envelope and saw Mia's passport and a plane ticket to Japan. She hugs Troy as he gives them his blessing. Anna rushes back to her room and told Mia the good news then they left for the airport. Big Jon, Troy, Leo, Marcus, Craig, Jerry, and Sam sat and talked for hours as the men get ready to go their separate ways. Big Jon asks them to stay a while and they all agree.

At the airport Carlos flight was delayed and he was moved to another flight. He sat there as he waits for his cell phone to charge. He looks at his new ring and an older gentleman sitting across from him recognized the custom-made, five carat blue diamond ring on Carlos's finger. He walks over to a pay phone and makes a call. He turns and walks towards Carlos, sitting next to him, making small talk. He leans in, looking Carlos in the eye, "Nice ring, my older brother has one like it."

Carlos reaches for his pen and clicks the stylus tip three times as the men talks more about the ring. Carlos tells the old man that he found the ring on the beach while he was on vacation. The old man laughs at Carlos "is this the vacation where you kill my son?" The airline customer services clerk walks over to Carlos and told him that she was able to get him on the next fight. Carlos smile at her "thanks you, do you like my ring? My friend here said it's a nice ring, and his brother has one like it. Here I thought I was the only one with this ring." Confused at what Carlos was talking about the clerk told him that it was a very nice ring. As she walks off, the old man gets up and whispers to Carlos "Get up, let's go for a walk," and they walked out of the airport together.

A few days later Jerry was sitting on the counter in the kitchen talking to Laura on the phone. Leo askes Jerry if he was talking to Carlos, Jerry got off the phone, "No, I haven't heard from him." Leo reaches for his cell phone and calls Carlos's cell phone, but the line was busy. Craig and Troy walks in on the conversation Leo yells for Sam and Marcus to come to the kitchen. He asks the team if anyone had heard from Carlos, they look at each other "no, we haven't heard from him, what's going on?"

Leo calls the number again the line was still busy, as the men stand around the phone, Leo puts the speaker on and calls the number again. The phone rings and rings and then a little voice answers the phone, "Uncle Leo?" The team looks at each other. Leo

yells "Junior?" the small gentle voice on the phone responds, "Yes…

Uncle Leo, my daddy never came home." The team stood in silence

as they look over at Leo in shock.

Chapter Nine

Leo puts the phone closer to his mouth as Troy, Marcus, Craig, and Sam remain quiet. They look at Leo in disbelief. Jerry paces the floor talking to himself "I should have left with him". As the leader of the team, Leo felt responsible for Carlos's disappearance. Leo calmly speaks, "Junior, where is your mom?"

Junior yells for his mom, she rushes to the phone with the baby in her hands. "Leo, Leo is that you?" Leo sigh with relief, "Yes, Maria where are you, are you safe?" Maria rubs Junior on the head "Yes, we are safe. Junior got a message from Carlos. I don't know what happen Leo, but I fear the worst." Jerry stumbles as he thinks the worst of his friend, "We are coming Maria, stay where you are!" he yells. Maria holds back her tears, "Yes, we will, Leo. Please hurry."

Junior takes the phone from his mom, "Uncle Leo, my dad left you a message, he said to tell you "Nice ring, my brother has one like it." The phone line went dead, Jerry grabs is head as Sam begins to pace the floor. Marcus, Craig, and Troy, look on speechless at

Leo. Troy walks to his office and he sits at his desk. As he unlocks his desk drawer, he looks at the gift that Carlos gave him. Troy decides to call Big Jon. After a somber greeting, he tells Jon the bad news.

While Leo tells his team to pack their bags, Troy walks in, "Let's not haste, we need to wait for Big Jon." Frustrated at the situation, Leo reminds Troy that this is his team, and they were leaving. Sam was concerned as he walks over to the team, "You heard Leo, let's get packing." Jerry, Craig, and Marcus looked at Troy sideways as they exit the kitchen.

Sam strolls over to Leo, he looks up at him, "I agree with Troy we should wait for Big Jon." Leo sits on the edge of the chair with his head down thinking of his next move. Sam leaves the room to pack their bags for the trip to Mexico. Troy joins Leo at the table with great concern. He reminds Leo of the sacrifices his team has made for him. "Leo, I know that this is your team there is no doubt about it. These men will die for you. My question is, how many men will you sacrifice?" Troy asked sternly.

With the loss of Leanna fresh in Leo's thoughts, he agrees with Troy and the team that they will wait patiently for Big Jon to arrive. Several hours later there was no sign of Big Jon and the team grew anxious as they waited for him. Jerry approaches Sam, "We are losing day light." Sam calmly tells Jerry, "We will do what Leo tells us to do." Suddenly, there was a loud knock at the back door. The maid walks over to open the door, but Troy hastily dismisses her. Troy opens the door and yells at the team, "Our ride is here!" He looks surprisingly at the private yacht that waits for them, he nods with approval.

The team made their way over to the yacht where Big Jon waits on their arrival. As the team walks up the ramp, they were greeted Big Jon. Then Troy's walks up the ramp and Big Jon acknowledge his present. Leo closely follows Troy up the ramp, then Big Jon stops him "I am not coming with you on this journey, here is where we part ways," he said in a stern voice. Leo felt overcome with emotion as he thought about everything big Jon had done for him. He never should have been so quick to dismiss the help that only this man could give. Big Jon exits the yacht and wave as they leave. Leo was confused of big Jon's decision to stay behind. Troy reminds Leo that big Jon is not as frail as he looks. The team went to their rooms while Leo, Sam and Troy gather in the dining room.

The maid approaches the three men, "The captain would like to meet with you," she said cordially. Sam points to himself, "Me ...?" he asks in confusion. She smiles warmly at him, "Yes, you are also welcome to the captain quarters. Please follow me," she said. As the maid walks off the three men follow her to the private room. She opens the door and announces their presence. She invites the men into the room, "Please make yourself at home." The maid exits the room and closes the door behind her.

In the dark room the captain sits at his desk, he speaks to the men, "You were so young when your dad died. Troy, I believe you were eleven and Leo you were eight. Now you all grown up," he mused. The captain sits in the shadows, with his face hidden. He tells them stories of the many adventures he had with their father, "Your father would be proud of you boys." he gushed. He thanks Sam for always being Leo's right hand.

The captain tells Leo that Big Jon left something in his care for him. He uses his cane to point to the big brown envelope on his desk. Leo picks up the envelope. Silently, the security guards enter the room, and the captain dismisses the men. They begin to walk out of the room and then the captain taps his cane; everyone turns around. "Leo I'm deeply sorry for your lost," Leo gives a stiff nod, and the men exit the captain's quarters as security escorts them to their own rooms.

In his room Leo sees his bags, he then sits on the bed. He opens the big brown envelope that Big Jon left him. There he sees a note from the wise man, he reads in silents, "Leo, Carlos gave me special instruction in case something happens to you. I think that you can use this information to find Carlos." Leo reads the letter in silence a few times, he sighs as he thinks of Carlos's family. Following the instruction in the letter, he looks at the black bracelet on his wrist that Carlos gave him. Again, he tries to remove the bracelet. He struggles to remove the bracelet, on the third try the bracelet constricts to his wrist causing Leo to fall to his knee in pain. Then the symbol of the lion flashes green and the bracelet releases as it adjusts to fit his wrist. Leo's phone rings and he answers, "Hello." The sound of loud static on the phone hurts Leo's ear. He could hear someone breathing on the phone. Leo looks at his phone, "Hello, who is this?" he yelled over the static.

A little voice comes from the phone, "Uncle Leo, I can see you." Leo gets up and walks over to the window, he closes the window curtain, "Junior…?" Junior's little voice trembles as he speaks, "Yes, I can see you," he said strongly. Leo looks at the bracelet on his wrist, "Junior, how can you see me?" Juniors tries to explain over the static on the phone, "I can see the lion on my game. You're in the water, so I click on the lion and your phone ring." Leo reaches and holds the window curtain. He looks out at the calm sea, "Junior, can you see uncle Jerry or Uncle Sam?" Leo closes the window curtain.

Junior intensely looks at his game monitor, "No, just you, just the lion". Leo paces in his room, "Junior, can you get your mom?" Junior runs to the kitchen to get his mom. Maria rushes to Juniors room excited to hear that Leo was on the phone. "Leo is that you! Can you hear me, it's Maria? Oh my god Leo, I can see you on the game, where are you?" she asked in surprise.

Leo calms her down, "Maria can Junior hear me?" She walks to the corner of the room, "No just me." Leo asks Maria to put the phone on speaker so that Junior can hear him. Leo runs to Sam's room and bangs on the door. Sam opens the door, ready to curse the one responsible for disturbing his peace when suddenly Leo grabs his arm and adjusts the watch. Sam falls to the floor in pain yelling at Leo. The light on the watch came on. Leo kisses Sam on the head as Sam looks on in disbelief. Leo askes Junior if he could see Sam now?

Junior yells excitedly, "Yes, I can see Uncle Sam's sniper gun." Sam looks at Leo; neither one could believe what they were seeing. He rushes to wake up Craig, Marcus, Troy, and Jerry, banging on their room doors. The men were all confused of Sam's behavior as they follow him to his room. "Junior can see us," he explained as he pushes everyone into his room. Leo tells Troy to adjust the bracelet that Carlos gave him Troy did as he was told. Junior was confused at what he saw, "I can't see Uncle Troy. I can only see a monkey."

The team laughs at Troy as he snatches the phone from Leo, "Junior that's a silverback, the true king of the jungle," he explained. Leo takes the phone from Troy as he pushes him out of the way. Sam tells Jerry, Craig, and Marcus to adjust the jewelry that Carlos gave them. While Junior and his mom stay on the phone, they let the team know when their matching avatar is seen on the game.

Jerry adjusts his neckless and Junior was able to see a bomb on his game. Marcus struggles to activate but manages one earring. Junior could see a part of a car. Marcus cries as he turns the other earring and Junior was able to see the entire car. Craig runs to his room to get the black lighter that Carlos gave him. He returns to Sam's room and strikes the lighter, but nothing happens. He strikes it a second time, and nothing happen. On the third try, he presses down, and holds the button on the lighter, and a big machine gun avatar pops up onto Junior's game. Leo told Junior that he did a great job and to go to bed. Leo ensures Maria that they are on their way and that he will not stop until he finds Carlos. He tells her to get ready for their trips. Maria begs Leo to hurry as she holds back her tears. That night, the team slept on the floor in Sam's room, while Sam enjoys the bed all to himself.

Meanwhile, Maria rushes to her room and begins to pack for their trip. She tells Junior to pack up and he did as he was told. Once he was all packed up, Junior sneaks off to this dad's office and took a big black box. He gently wraps his clothing around the box and puts it in his bookbag. Then he heard something outside by the window. He looks up and sees a flashlight shining into the office. Junior crawls back to his mother's room and told his mother that someone was outside the window. Maria grabs her bags, she gently picks up her daughter, strapping the baby to her body. Then they heard the office window breaks. She looks through the crack of her room door and saw that Carlos's office was on fire. Junior pulls at his mother's arm, and points to the next room. He throws the laundry basket of t-shirts on the bed and uses the water from the large flower vase to wet them. He looks at his mother as he wraps the shirt around this face, only exposing his eyes. Then he wraps his mother face and covers his sister head with the other shirts.

Making their way over to the dark hallway, through the open doors, they heard a loud explosion on the lower level of their home. The force of the explosion causes Maria to lose her balance. With quick reflex, Junior reaches out and grabs his mother as she stumbles. Helping her to her feet, he held onto to his mother's hand. He whispers to her "follow me." As they made their way down the smoked filled stairs. Junior tightened his grip on his mother's hand. Holding her hand, he puts her hand on the wall. Using the wall to guide them as they slowly disappear into the smoke-filled room.

Chapter Ten

Jerry wakes up. He crawls over Craig and Marcus, waking them up as he makes his way to the couch. Sam wakes up smiling, "Such a soft bed" Jerry throws a pillow at him. He then turns and begins to kick at Craig poking him with his big toe, "Wake up," he said as he continued poking. Eventually, Craig got up and the team went to their room to get ready for the day. Leo looks out on the water as he thinks about Carlos's family.

In that moment he notices that the yacht has stopped. Leo walks down the hall to go to the captain's quarters, but the guards stop him, "He's not in there. Come, I'll take you to him." Leo follows the guards. Leo shields his face from the bright sun as they make their way topside of the yacht. The guard stops, "This is as far as we can take you," he says. Leo looks down and sees his team as they are getting into a boat, he follows his team.

The boat takes them to the island. There they notice that they were in Pachuca Mexico. The team walks the streets and finds a motel for the night. Leo goes to the office to make the arrangements.

They decided to make the bar their official rendezvous point. Troy's tells the team to wash up and meet back at the spot in one hour.

Leo walks over to the team he hands them the key to their rooms. Craig looks at the map on his phone, "It looks like we are eleven hours from Durango, and the only way to get there is by car." Jerry looks at his phone, "Did anyone hear from Junior today?"

Sam quickly answers, "Junior is a smart boy, I'm sure he is okay." Everyone parted ways and went back to their rooms. They met at the bar in exactly one hour. Sam went up to the counter and ordered dinner for the team. As they sit and eat, they plan about their next move. Craig went to the restroom and overheard a man as he talks about Durango. Pretending to leave, Craig stands at the end of the hallway as he listens to the men. He remains unseen as he watches the men exit the bathroom, he quickly buys the men a drink and sits with them for a while.

The team eat their dinner. As they wait for Craig, Marcus orders another round of drinks. Craig comes back to the table and tells the team that he got them a ride from a kid to Durango, but they would have to leave tonight. The team agrees to the plan. The driver walks over to Craig and tells him it's time to go. Then he interduces his self as Rico to the team. As the team left in the night for

Durango, Leo sits in the front of the van and checks his phone to see if Junior called.

He has not heard from Junior that entire day, and he was getting worried. Rico looks at Leo, "Why the sad looks on your face my friend, you're in Mexico it's time to party." Leo looks out the window just as Rico pulls into the resort. He hits Troy, "Get up, look," he points to the resort. Troy wakes the rest of the team. Rico pulls to the back of the resort, "Let's stretch our legs," he says as he exits the van and disappears into the dark. The team remains seated in the van.

Jerry looks out the window of the van, "I don't like this" he mutters. Just then, he sees an old man walking their way. Singling the crew, Jerry points at the old man. The old man approaches, and he hits the van, "Took you long enough," he said grumpily. Troy opens the door and sees Big Jon as he walks up to the door, the team hugs him with excitement. Soon, Big Jon was leading the way into the hotel and to his presidential suite. Big Jon explains to the team that he flew in because he gets seasick and that he sent his friends' son Rico, to the bar to find them.

Suddenly, Leo's phone rings and he quickly answers the call from the unknown number, "Hello!" Junior tries to adjust his game,

"Uncle Leo?" Leo takes a few steps, "Junior are you okay?" he asked worriedly. The static on the phone line drowned out Junior's voice, "Yes." Maria gets on the phone, panic-stricken "Leo some men came to our home, and they burned everything!" she cried. Leo walks to the other side of the room he tells Maria that they were close and will be there in the morning.

Maria tells Leo that she is staying with her Auntie Liz and that Junior's game was destroyed in the fire. Fortunately, Junior can still use the small game, but it is also broken. Big Jon interrupts the conversation "Leo, we need to go now" Leo tells Maria that they are on their way and to be ready to go when they arrive. Maria rushes to pack. The team gets in the Van and Rico drove through the night.

As the team arrives to Auntie Liz's home, Big Jon tells Jerry and Leo to go to the house and get Maria and her children. Rico tells Jerry to pull up the rug on the floor of the van and slide the wood. There Jerry found guns. He smiles as he hands them out to the team. Craig, Jerry, and Marcus watch the streets, big Jon tells Rico and Troy to be ready for anything. Leo and Jerry approach the front of the home. Auntie Liz opens the doors with a bat in her hand, she sees that it was Leo and Jerry, and she invites the men inside. Maria runs over to Leo; she hugs and kisses him then she embraces Carlos's best friend Jerry. Junior hides behind the table as he looks at the men, he remembers the stories his dad told him about his uncles. Maria filled with excitement; she yells "Junior come meet your uncles." Junior was shy as he approaches his uncles, he keeps a distance from them. Auntie Liz goes and gets the baby from her room. Leo tells Auntie Liz that she is not safe here and that she should come with them, and she agrees. Leo asks Junior to see his game, Junior slowly walks over, he pulls out his hand-held game out of his backpack and hands it to Leo.

Leo inspects the game, looking it over, "Junior, I'll fix the screen for you so you can see us," he promises. Junior takes the game and puts it back into his bag and smiles. Leo walks with him to the van. Rico makes a call and the team heads to the Chicken Ranch in Durango. At the ranch a red headed woman and her maid waits for the team to arrive. Big Jon introduces the team to his friend Katrina and her maid Sofia. Junior asks to see Katrina's chickens. Big Jon whispers to Junior, "This is an old ranch, and that Katrina is only old hen left around here."

Katrina was a woman of the world, and she was well known among the men in the army. She kisses big Jon and Rico as she welcomes the team into her home. Katrina was excited to have visitors. She tells Sofia to watch the kids as she shows Maria and Auntie Liz their rooms. As the kids play with her cats, Katrina turns to Maria, "This must be very serious for Big Jon to put my son at risk." Maria thanks her for welcoming them into her home. Katrina turns to Maria, "I lost my home a long time ago," as she walks out of the room. Katrina calls Leo over to her, she holds his face in her hands as she looks at him, "You have your father's face, and I can see the pain in your eyes."

Troy walks over as he interrupts their conversation. Katrina turns to Troy, "And you have your father's manners." She yells at them, "Follow me!" She gets in the gulf cart and rides to the barn where the team awaits. Katrina shows the team the barn and gives a quick tour. She takes them to an elevator, and they go down to the basement of the barn. Katrina shows the team their rooms.

Craig elbows Sam, "She's hot, I think I'm in love." Sam rolled his eyes. As Katrina opens the door to the ammunition room, Jerry was in heaven when he sees all the guns and bombs lining the walls. He kisses Marcus on his cheek as they run to the guns. Leo asks Katrina if she could get Junior's game fixed so that he could continue checking for any clues in Carlos's disappearance. Katrina calls Rico and tells him to bring Junior and his game to her.

Junior walks into the room where he sees Katrina and the rest of the team. Scared, he runs over to his uncle Leo and holds his hand. Leo sits on the floor and interduces Junior to everyone on the team. The team comes up to Junior and shakes his hand. Junior had heard so many stories about his dad's team that he looks at the men with amazement. He smiles as Marcus gives him a high five. Then Junior hands Katrina the game and she takes it from him.

She held Junior's little hand in hers, "Junior, I want show you something," she said. She takes the key from around her neck and unlocks the door to her panic room. Junior eyes got big as he looks at the computer systems, cameras, and the televisions in the massive room. Katrina whispered to Junior, "This is your room." Smiling, he runs to the computer and looks at the different systems as he digs though the drawers, picking up supplies. Leo walks over to him, "Did you find anything that can fix your game Junior?" he asked, as he sits on the floor. Junior unscrews the Gameboy and remove a chip from the device. The team looks at him in disbelief.

Junior crawls under the desk and removes the hard drive from the system and installs the chip from his game to Katrina's system. He rushes to the chair and logs into the game. Right there on the screen the Lion, the silverback, the race car, the bomb, the sniper, and the machine gun came to life. Junior clicks through the file and the team could see their kill score, weakness, strengths, and their weapon of choice. Big Jon looks on with a shocked look on his face, "Junior did your dad create this game for you?" he asked.

Junior points to the screen, "That's daddy." Leo takes a closer look at the screen, and he sees a keyboard. He asks Junior if that light ever flashes on the keyboard. Junior pulls up a new map on the screen as he shows the team old videos of the keyboard. The adults look on as the shy ten-year-old navigates throughout his game.

Katrina pulls a chair over and begins to help Junior, he smiles as she shows him how to move and rotate the camera to see the different directions of the keyboard. Katrina points to the screen with excitement, "There, this is the last location of the keyboard, it's on a farm, about forty minutes from here."

Junior watches the screen intensely, as Katrina continues to tell the team about the farm. "This farm is where people go to work, they work these people to death, no one ever gets out alive." She continues to tell that the farm is mostly known for the abundance of different kind of produce and that their specialty is meat. Jerry walks over to Leo, he whispers "This is where Carlos is? You know he's a smart man, he would have made it home by now." Leo agrees with him as they wonder what Carlos was up too.

Chapter Eleven

Katrina orders the team to go back to the main house and get some rest, she sits with Junior for a while. She gives Junior a new Gameboy and copies the game from the system. She tells Junior, "I am your friend and I want you to help me to understand. Junior did your dad teach you about computers?" She turns his chair as she holds his wrist "How old are you?" she asked. Junior pulls his hand away from Katrina and askes to use the bathroom. "Let me show you a little secret." Katrina said.

Katrina opens the coat closet as she held Junior's hand. They walk through the dim light to the main house. She tells Junior, "This is our little secret. Don't tell anyone, not even your mommy." Junior nods at her as they exit the dim lights as they walk-through Katrina's office in the main house. In the kitchen Maria, Sofia, and Liz made dinner for the team. As they sit down to eat, Leo fills in Maria and the team on what they should do. At sunrise, Big Jon will head out to buy some meat from the farm. He will bring Rico with him since he knows the area.

Katrina was not happy with this arraignment, so she requests for Marcus to go with them. Maria gets up and walks over to Rico. She takes off her handmade rose cross neckless that Carlos gave her. Leo reaches for the cross. He takes a long look at it and presses the rose in the middle of the cross and the rose turns red. Suddenly, Junior's game beeps. He takes it out of his jacket and sees a heart on screen, "Mommy you're in the game!" squealed Junior with delight. As he shows his mom, Katrina smiles at Junior.

The team went to their room in the barn while Rico and Big Jon stays in the main house with Katrina, Maria and her two children, Sofia, and Liz. This was the best night sleep the team had in a long time. In the morning the team went to the main house to finalize their plans. As Big Jon, Rico and Marcus gets ready to leave, Leo tells Maria, Sofia, and Liz to stay in the barn, Maria leaves to get her children, and they made their way over to the barn. In the barn the rest of the team set up as they wait patiently.

Junior and Katrina logon to the computer and begin to track Rico, Big Jon, and Marcus. Leo asks to speak with Jerry, Craig, Sam, and Troy in private. He was concerned that Rico would not be able to protect the team. He tells Jerry and Craig to follow Rico at a distance and keep him updated. Troy nods in agreement with Leo.

Rico drove while Big Jon sits in the passenger seat. Marcus sits in the back of the truck, and he checks in with Leo as the truck approaches the farm.

At the barn, Maria sits with her daughter as her son and Katrina track the team. Katrina tells Maria that her son is a genius like his grandfather. Maria was confused, she looks at Katrina, "How do you know Carlos's father?" Katrina looks at Maria and smiles, "A girl never kisses and tells," she says sweetly, turning towards the monitor. Junior watches the screen for Carlos's location.

Big Jon, Marcus, and Rico pull up to the farms gate and they were told to park the truck. The guard walks over and asks Big Jon what kind of supplies he needed. He tells the guard that he is having a party and he needs some produce and meat. Big Jon pulls out his shopping list from his pocket. Intentionally dropping a large amount of cash on the ground. To show that he was a wealthy man. The guard picks up the money and tells Big Jon that he came to the right place. He smiled as he hands Big Jon his money. A gesture to show Big Jon that the establishment was honest.

Upon seeing the large amount of money, one of the guards walk over from behind the heavy steel gated. He walks up to the truck and looks inside of Big Jon's truck. He smirks at Rico, who was nervously sitting in the driver's seat. The guard kicks the front tire of the truck and Rico jumped. The guard smiles as he repeatedly nods his head, he strolls to the back of the truck. As he looks in the back of the open truck, he sized up Marcus. Marcus sits quietly with his head hanging down. The guard walks over to Big Jon, as he adjusted his gun around his waist he said, "Tell your boys to wait here while I show you around." Big Jon yells at Marcus and Rico to stay in the truck. The guard then interduces himself to Big Jon as Nacho.

He asked Big Jon "what kind of produce is you looking to buy today, my friend?" Big Jon quickly replies, "whatever is in season, my friend." Big Jon tells Nacho that he heard that this farm has the best meat in town. Nacho laughs as he escorts Big Jon through the massive steel gates "you heard right my friend." As they made their way over to the butcher shop. Marcus watches from inside the back of the truck while Rico pretends to work on the truck's engine. After walking the grounds of the farm for about two hours there was nothing left for Jon to see. The guard walks Big Jon over to the desk, where he pays for his items. He notices several women and children on the farm. Jokingly he asked the cashier, "Are they for sale too?"

Nacho smiles, "Yes, everything on the farm is for sale." Big Jon smiles at Nacho, "Oh, very nice" as he nods his head. Nacho seeing Big Jon's reaction he decides to invite Big Jon inside to meet the owner. Big Jon quickly accepted the invitation. Once inside, Nacho told one of the women that was sitting with the children as they play to bring their guest a cold glass of lemonade. Then he signals Big Jon to have a seat. Big Jon walks over to the brown wooden chair and sits. He looks around as he takes off his hat, resting it on his knee as the woman approaches with his drink. Her bruised handshakes as she hands him the drink. Big Jon takes the drink and stirs it in his glass as she runs back over to the children. Other guards walk into the room and whispers to Nacho. He quickly excuses himself as they exit the room.

Big Jon sits on the wooden stool patiently as the sound of children playing echoes through the room. He looks at the drink and discards the lemonade into a nearby plant. Nacho returns with the owner of the farm who introduces himself as Juan. The two men sit and talk for a while. Juan whispers to Nacho, "Bring the inventory, only the best for our guest." Nacho signals the other guard, and they left the room and later returned with four young girls and four young boys.

Big Jon stares at the scene, disturbed by this display of the young children. Concealing his distaste, he smiles slyly. He put his hat on "A little too young for me. I like them a little older and strong, just like my boys out front."

Nacho smiles in understanding, "I might have something for you," he said. The guard walks to the other room and returns with three men. Jon looks in horror at the men, "Too tall," he says, signaling he was not interested in the current wares. He gets up and tucks his shirt into his pants. The owner askes Big Jon to sit. He turns to Nacho and whispers, "Bring the troublemaker," as he smiles. Nacho rushes out the room and did what he was told. Big Jon sits and patiently waits for him to return. Juan begins to tell Big Jon that this new boy was wild and hard to train. Soon, Nacho and two others guard returns to the room with a man in tow. Big Jon looks up and sees Carlos.

He smiles, "Perfect, in every way." Juan saw that Big Jon really wanted this house boy. He tells Jon that this house boy is very, very expensive and that he found him wondering the street. Big Jon reaches into his pocket and pulls out a large stack of money. Juan tells Big Jon that this was not enough for this special house boy. He is untouched, as he walks over putting his hand on Carlos's shoulder.

Big Jon reaches into his socks and pulls out another stack of money. This makes Juan smile widen. Big Jon askes the house boy his name. When he did not answer, Jon strikes him with his cane. Juan, Nacho, and the rest of the guards laugh at the house boy as they praise Big Jon for his stern hand. Juan yells for the maid to bring him two beers to celebrate the sale and his new friend. The maid walks over slowly. She was wearing all black and no one could see her face, hands, or feet. Big Jon could tell that she was hiding something. He uses his cane to lift-up her chin so that he could see her face. Just then, Juan yells at the maid to get back to the kitchen. He looks at Big Jon, "This one is not for sale; she belongs to my cousin's son. Once he gets what he wants than I will have her."

Big Jon drinks the beer. Escorted by Nacho he went back to his truck to wait for the other guards to bring him his new purchases. In the dark, the guard brings Big Jon all the produce items he paid for, but not the house boy. Big Jon asks one of the guards "where is my house boy, what is taking so long" the guard tells Big Jon the special house boy is a hard one to train. Big Jon points at Marcus who was sitting by his feet, "So was this one, now look at him." Marcus kept his head down. Big Jon started to grow angry with the guard. Upon seeing this display of anger, Nacho signals for the guard to bring the house boy.

Back at the barn, Leo waits for Jerry and Craig to check in and he grows impatient. Unable to wait any longer, he decided to go check on his friends and Troy agrees to go with him. Leo orders Sam to stay behind and to keep watch of the barn. Leo and Troy got in the jeep and headed for the farm. A few minutes later, Jerry calls Leo's phone. Leo pulls over to answer and Jerry tells Leo, "We are about 2 miles from the farm, the security is tight." Leo puts the call on speaker, "Can you see Big Jon or Marcus?" he asks.

Jerry sighs, "No, we can't see what's going on and there is no movement on the roads."

This was not the news that Leo and Troy wanted to hear. Troy yells at the phone, "We are on the way." Jerry told them to hang tight and not come. He ensures Leo that he will check back in a few, then he hangs up the phone. Leo and Troy sit in the jeep anxiously waiting for Jerry to call back.

Chapter Twelve

Back at the farm Big Jon's patience grows to anger as he waits for his new house boy. Then in a distance he sees two guards carrying Carlos by his hands and feet. They throw him in the back of the truck. Marcus jumps in the back of the truck and helps the guards to secure Big Jon's special purchase. Carlos was laid out unconscious in the back of the truck. Big Jon yells at Nacho, "Is he dead?"

Juan laughs as he strolls over to Nacho. He looks up at Big Jon "No, just sleeping. The fool would rather stay here than be a house boy for an old fool like you," he quipped, and the guards laugh at Big Jon. Big Jon hits the top of the truck with his cane and with that, Rico turns on the engine and begins to drive, exiting the farm in a hurry.

That night Rico drove like a mad man. He flew past Jerry and Craig as they look on. They could only see Marcus in the back of the truck. Fearing the worst, they started to drive behind them. A few miles down the road Leo and Troy started to grow impatient. They decided that they would wait no longer for Jerry and Craig to call. As they were about to start making his way to the farm Troy sees Rico's truck in a distance. As they speed past them, Leo made the tight turn and followed the truck. He sees Jerry and Craig Jeep coming up quickly behind them and he knew something was wrong. Troy calls Sam who quickly answers the phone, "There is an emergency, Big Jon's on the way, open the gates."

Sam runs to the computer monitor and told Katrina to open the gates. They watch the monitor as the team approaches the gate. As the cars pulls into the unlevel driveway, Sam and Katrina runs to the main house. Rico pulls in and they all jump out the truck helping Marcus as they bring Carlos into the main house. Leo, Troy, Jerry, and Craig pull up and quickly enter the house. There, they see Carlos laying on the floor. Big Jon tells Leo to get the green and white bag and sends Katrina to get some medical supplies. Katrina and Leo rushes back to the front room with the items and Big Jon starts an IV bag to flush the drugs from Carlos's system.

Maria waits at the barn with her children and her auntie Liz when she hears the commotion over at the big house. With her baby in her arms, she grabs Junior by the collar of his shirt and went running to the main house, Liz follows behind her in the darkness of the night. She tears into to the main house through the side door. She rushes to the front room and fell to the floor crying as she looks over and sees Carlos laying on the floor. Jerry and Craig quickly took her and the children to the upper room where Liz sits and prays with them.

A few hours later, the team sits around Carlos as he lays on the couch when suddenly, he begins to cough. Big Jon tells Marcus to bring warm water and Big Jon makes Carlos some herbal tea. Leo helps Carlos to sit up and drink the tea, he takes a few sips of the eat and asks if his family was okay. Leo tells him that they are here in the upper room. "Don't let them see me like this," Carlos tells Leo. He tries to stand and stumbling to the floor, Leo, and Sam catches him. Big Jon signals for them to bring their downed comrade to the other room. Leo and Sam slowly walk Carlos to the next room, and they lay him on the bed as Katrina follows behind them with blankets in her hand.

Big Jon turns to the rest of the team and tells them that Carlos was drugged with different kinds of medication and that he should rest for the night. Katrina looks on as Carlos lays on the bed. Sofia walks in with an overside bowl of warm water. Katrina tells her to go fine some clean clothes for him. Katrina gently washes his body the best she could and dresses his wounds. The team sit in the dining room. Big Jon sits at the head of the table as he tells the team about the vile things he saw at the farm. As Leo and Troy walks in, Big Jon looks over at them as he continues telling the team about the strong effort, he had to make to conceal his disgust with the items that Juan had on display. His gauzed become wary as he speaks, "That place must be burned to the ground and Juan and this guards must pay" as he clenches his teeth Troy nods in agreement.

In that moment, Katrina walks over to the group, "Carlos is up, and he want to speak to all of you." she says. The team gets up and goes to see Carlos in his room, Carlos gathers his strength as he sits up in the bed, "I wanted to stay on the farm, those people need me, I was helping to keep them safe." Big Jon looks at him questioningly, "Why would you risk your life?" he asks baffled. Carlos positions himself in the bed as he tells the team that he was helping the slaves to escape.

Carlos tells his team what happen to him at the airport and how he was able send his location to Junior's game. He looks over at Leo, "I knew you would take care of my family and you would find me." Leo crosses his arms as he listens to his friend's weak voice. Carlos told them all about Luke's father Eli, and that he was on the way to the party when his sister-in-law called him. He could hear as Luke screamed and begged for his life. That's when the old man decided to return to the airport. Carlos stared off into the distance, "He noticed the ring on my finger because he personally made the ring for his younger brother," he told them as he touched his finger.

Carlos continues to tell the team about how he was able to escape from Eli but was soon found by Juan as he wondered the roads. Carlos tells the team that he heard that Eli often visits the farm. He has a thing for younger man and the farm keeps him fully supplied Carlos coughs. He reaches for his tea and takes a few sips of his warm tea, "He will stop at nothing until he gets his revenge. There is something else on the farm that Eli comes to check on. This was a special gift that Luke gave him" he says with a deep breath. Carlos turns and puts his cup of tea on the nightstand, he looks at Leo, "If we take this gift, then Eli will come to us."

Leo walks over to Carlos's bed, "We will make them pay for what they did to you," he promised. Katrina interrupt and tell them that this was enough for one night and asks the team to leave so that Carlos could get some rest. Carlos's ask Leo to stay a while once everyone exits his room. Once alone Carlos looks at Leo, "The girl in all black, they call her Bella. She is carrying Luke's child. Bella is of the most vital importance to Eli since she is carrying the last of his blood line." Carlos points to the note pad on the desk. Leo picks it up and gave it to him. Carlos begins to draw maps, giving detailed information on the layout of the farm. There was no rest that night as the team worked diligently to strategize a plan to get Bella.

Carlos asks Leo to bring back Troy, Jerry, Craig, Marcus, and Sam to the room. Leo leaves and returns with the rest of the team assembling in the room. Carlos waited once he had everyone's attention and told the team that this cannot be a rush job. Eli will be visiting the farm in three days, and this will give the team the time they need to prepare. With this decided, Carlos then asks to see his family. Jerry breaks into a run as he sets of to get Maria and the kids. He runs up the stairs with loud, booming steps. Big Jon hears the running and thinking the worst, he rushes to the room with his emergency bag.

Maria and the kids rush to his room, and she embrace her husband with the children in her arms. The team exits the room so the family could be alone. Carlos tells Maria how much he loves her as he kisses his daughter. He holds Junior in his arms, "My little genius, I knew you would find your uncles and lead them to me," he said with praise, kissing his head. That night Maria and the kids slept in Carlos's room. Maria sees the bruises on his body as she watches him sleep through the night.

While Carlos and his family settle in for the night. The team gathers in the kitchen discussing the farm and making plans on how to handle the situation. Troy tells the team that this cannot be a rush job. Leo chimes in "everyone should get some rest, you heard Carlos we have three days" He walks off to his room. As the team went to their rooms Leo sit alone in his room. He thinks of his Leanna and their son, that night he dreams about the first time he met Leanna.

In his room Big Jon, tosses and turn the entire night, he could not sleep. He gets up and reaches for this phone calling Anna in secret. The phone rings and rings; there was no answer. Big Jon turns off the light and went to sleep. In the morning Katrina, made breakfast for everyone as the team gather around the kitchen table. Maria and Carlos walk in with their children. The team get up out of their chairs and applaud the family They all sit at the table and have a big breakfast. They eat, drink, and enjoy this moment together. Leo looks at his team and thanks them for everything they have done for him. The team raises their glasses and make cheers to Leo for being a great leader as Troy hugs his brother.

Later that day Big Jon tells the team to train as he meets with Troy. Concerned about the manpower on the farm, Big Jon tells Troy that they will need some help, people they know and trust. Troy agrees with Big Jon. He walks off to get some privacy as he calls the silverbacks nest and tells his most trusted guard Sean to be on standby. Troy tells Sean to make all the necessary arrangements for the ten best silverbacks guards to be in Mexico by the second day. Sam, Jerry, Marcus, and Craig train in the fields by the barn. Junior, filled with excitement, shows his dad the panic room and the changes he made to it.

Leo sneaks off to his room where he sits on the bed thinking of the risk Carlos took. Carlos tells Junior to go help Katrina as he goes looking for Leo. He walks to the main house, meandering through the halls to Leo's room. Carlos knocks on the door, "Leo, you in there?" Leo sits up in the bed, "Yes, come in." Carlos walks in and sits down next to Leo on the bed. The two sit together for hours as they talk more about the farm. Leo listened intently as Carlos told him about his time on the farm and how it changes people. Carlos tells Leo, "Juan was right about one thing, I'm unbreakable." Leo asks Carlos, "What did they do to you?"

Carlos looks at Leo, "Everything, and yet they could not break me. I had to stay alive for you," he said somberly. Leo looks at Carlos, in that moment he understood why he gave the team their gifts. Just outside the door, Maria stood listening. After a long day, the team settles into their rooms as they get ready for the fight of their lives. That night Maria made love to Carlos as she fell in love with him all over again.

Big Jon and Katrina spend the night talking about the old days in the army. Katrina tells Big Jon that Troy, Leo, and Rico are brothers, and Rico was the reason why their dad, Ethan, died. With a sigh of relief Katrine tells Big Jon that Ethan sacrificed himself so that his unborn child could live. She went on to tell Jon that Juan was the one who pulled the trigger, taking their father's life. Juan was going to kill his daughter because she was carrying a gringo's child.

Katrina promises Ethan on his death bed that she would protect them both and when Rico's mother died in childbirth. Katrina raises him as her son, she begs Big Jon "take care of Rico." Big Jon convinces Katrina to tell Leo and Troy the truth about their father's killer and their little brother. Katrina agrees that it is time for the brothers to know the truth. That night, Big Jon and Katrina kept each other company.

Chapter Thirteen

In the morning Katrina, Maria, and Liz were in the kitchen making breakfast. While Sofia took care for the baby, Big Jon calls the entire team to the kitchen. While the team sat and ate their breakfast, Big Jon stood up to speak to everyone when there was a knock at the door. Troy rushes to answer the door. He smiles when he opens it and sees Anna and Mia standing before him, they walk in, hugging Troy and the rest of the team. Big Jon was surprised to see them. He pushes Jerry out of his way and hugs Anna, "You got my messages!" he claimed.

Anna smiled, "Yes, and Troy's too." She greets Leo as Mia hugs him. Anna grabs a slice of bacon, "Here I am, fill me in." Mia sits at the table and starts to prepare Anna's plate. Big Jon stood up and he explained to Anna and Mia what happened to Carlos and what there were planning to do tomorrow night. Now that Anna and Mia were all caught up, he gave the floor to Katrina. With tears in her eyes, she told the brothers that they were not alone. Katrina went on to tell the story of Ethan's bravery and death. She told Leo and Troy that the Chicken Farm is belongs to their father and is rightfully theirs. Holding back her tears, she tells the brother that many years ago, their father bought this farm in hopes of raising his three sons here.

Leo and Troy look at each other. Leo sits back in his chair, "There's just two of us, Ethan only had two sons!" Katrina looks at the bothers gravely and continued to tell Leo and Troy that Rico is their younger brother. She explained how their father came to Mexico to get Rico's mother and bring her to the United States. When Juan found out about this, he tried to kill his daughter, but he shot Ethan instead. She pulls out an old letter that their dad wrote to the brothers. Sam reaches for the letter and reads it out loud:

To my sons Troy and Leo, you have a baby brother that I hope you will meet someday. Troy, I want to you to look after your brothers. Most of all I want you to know that I did not leave you. To find your brother you must see the chicken farm. Leo, please try and remember where you drove alone for the first time. Even though I'm not with you, I will continue to watch over my three boys!

Dad.

Leo looks over at Troy, "Dad took me to the OCIR racetrack when I was seven and told me to drive," he said. Troy laughs, "Yeah, I remember that day. You cried like a little bitch." Sam gives Leo the letter, "Leo, OCIR spelled backwards is RICO." Troy looks over at Rico, "He does kind of look like a weaker version of you Leo," he said squinting his eyes.

Leo walks over the Katrina, "Who killed our dad?" he demanded. Katrine turns and looks Leo in his eyes, "Juan," she confessed. Leo tells the team to continue their training. Katrina gets up and kisses Rico on the head. She tells Anna and Mia to follow her as she shows them to their rooms. Big Jon told the brothers that Ethan's blood flows through their veins and that nothing or anyone can change that. He ensures the brothers that Katrina is many things, but she is not a liar, and that Katrina is a woman that keeps her word.

The brothers agree that they will let Juan pay for what he has done to their father. Big Jon walks out of the kitchen and over to the training area. While the three brother looks at each other in silents. Rico breaks the silent and speaks to his brother for the first time, "When I was a kid, Katrina use to tell me stories of the silverback and the Lion and the God that created them both. Now I know that that God was my father, Ethan." He sits back and puts his hands in his pockets, "I know that you don't see me as a brother, but I hope we can be brothers someday." He gets up and walks out the door to go train with the rest of the team. Leo and Troy look at each other, and the brothers sit in silence for a few. Troy remembers that their dad had told him about his baby brother. He looks at Leo, "All this time I thought he was talking about you, but now I understand that he was talking about Rico."

Leo and Troy slowly stroll to the training grounds as they watch Rico. Rico went for the knife and the axe just like Leo and their dad. He was also ambidextrous, just like his brothers. As they observe Rico's movement, they could each see themselves in him. They call Rico over to them. Excited, he breaks into a run as he joins them and the three brother practices together. Anna and Mia walk over to the training site. Anna looks over and sees the brothers training together, she smiles. Seeing Anna's reaction to this, Mia reaches for her hand and Anna kisses Mia, "It's time for mama to train," she says lovingly to Mia. Anna walks off to train as Mia goes to help Katrina clean up the kitchen. Carlos smiles at the brothers as they work and train together moving as one. Carlos watches them as the three brothers mimic each other. Big Jon could see their father in the brothers. Troy had their father's strength, Leo had his spirit, and Rico had his bravery.

Carlos left the training grounds and went to get his son Junior. Junior was in his room playing with his toys. He looks up and sees his dad, grabs his bookbag and leaves with his dad. Carlos took

Junior to the barn, where they log on the computer system. Carlos

looks over at Junior "you ready?" Junior nods and his dad begin to

train him. He told Junior that he will be helping with tracking the

team tomorrow night. Junior looks at his dad as he opens his

bookbag, "Dad, I was able to save some of your kits." Junior pulls

out a brown paper bag with microchips, nanorobotics, and the black

box. Proud of his son Carlos hugs and kisses Junior's head as they

start to work on building more tracking devices. A few hours later

Troy Left the training site and went to his room, as he sits alone in

his room, he remembers the talk Big Jon had with him. He calls Sean

and tells him to send back-up to his location. Sean calls a meeting at

the silverback's nest and assembles the silverback's team.

Chapter Fourteen

After an intense day of training the team took a long hot bath
and got ready for dinner. As they gather and talk among themselves
everyone looks exhausted as they get ready to sit for dinner. They sit
around the dining room table, enjoying each other's company. Sam
raises his glass to toast to the three brother and the bright future for
their team. "Cheers!" they all exclaim. Maria, Mia, Katrina, and
Sofia made dinner for everyone, and they begin to serve the team.
Talking among themselves and making playful jokes with each
other. Big Jon looks on with a stern face, as he wonders if the team
was truly ready for their biggest assignment. Leo sees the concerned
look on Big Jon's face and he leans over to Jon, "Don't worry about
tomorrow. Let's just enjoy tonight," he says knowingly.

Big Jon nods in agreements with Leo, "Let's eat." Sofia
walks over to Leo to pours him a glass of wine. Leo hurried covering
his glass with his hand, "We will not drink any alcohol tonight," he
declared. Everyone turns their wine glass down and Sofia pours them
water instead of wine. That night big Jon and Katrina told their war

stories and the fun times they had with Ethan. The kids were getting sleepy, Sofia took Maria and Carlos's children to bed. Troy thanks Katrina for everything she had done to care for their brother Rico. Leo looks over at Rico as he takes a drink of his water, "We are all we have now." As the night come to an end, Carlos told the team to go get some rest. Maria, Mia, and Katrina begin to clear the table and tidy up for the night.

Anna, Craig, Marcus, Jerry, and Sam sat and listened intently while Carlos and Big Jon went over the final plans. Carlos told Leo that he must be the one to retrieve Luke's girlfriend and no one else. Carlos went on to tell the team that Luke's father has her well protected since she is carrying Luke's child. Carlos sighs, "Bella only gets to go outside once a day and she is always surrounded by many securities guards and at least two maids. Her personal doctor only comes once a month for check-ups, and he is not allowed to be alone with her. Troy, Sam, and Rico will be your back up. This will not be an easy grab and run, plus the farm goes on for miles and who knows what else is out there," he said breaking down the obstacles.

Big Jon gets up from the table; he glanced over at Carlos. Carlos looks away as if he was hiding something from the team. Big

Jon taps his cane and tells the brothers, "Get some rest for tomorrow your bonds will be tested." Big Jon, Craig, Anna, Jerry, Marcus, and Sam get up and tell each other good night as they went off to their rooms. Leo, Troy, Rico, and Carlos remain at the table and sit together in silence. Rico breaks the silence, he jokingly asks, "So what does a little brother do around here?"

Carlos throws a piece of bread at Rico. He catches it and eats it, laughing at Carlos. Carlos's reflects on the farm, he stares at Leo, "The farm changes people, it can make good people bad and bad people good. When you walk in there tomorrow you will see things that will haunt you for the rest of your life," he said with a serious look on his face. He gets up and tells his friends good night. Leo walks up and hugs him good night. Leo walks out of the dining room and retires to his room for the night. Carlos stops Troy and Rico from leaving he tells them, "Make sure no harm comes to Bella. She is a very precious package and Leo must be the only one to retrieve this special package. Protect Leo and make sure everyone gets out alive."

Troy's phone rings and he walks out and answer the call. Rico stares at Carlos, "I was always told that you were the more likeable one in the group. What did they do to you in there?" he asks.

Carlos looks at his trembling hands, "For their sport and entertainment, they made us fight to the death in front of the women and children. Then they made us eat the raw flesh of the ones we killed. The meat that we didn't eat Juan and his guards sells to the public," he recounted gravely.

Rico was disturbed by this. "How many men did you kill?" he asks Carlos. He looks up at Rico, "Ten men for hurting a child. One child that was suffering, three men that tried to rape me, and five of Juan's guards as I try to escape with Bella. Tomorrow you will see another side of your brothers and then you will understand all the stories that you were told about us. I hope that tomorrow you will rise to your calling." Carlos walks out of the dining room leaving Rico speechless as he wonders if his brothers are worth dying for.

Chapter Fifteen

Big Jon woke up early that morning and made a special breakfast for the team to prepare for the day's events. He goes thru the house, knocking on the team's room doors, alerting everyone it was time to get ready. Once the team was dressed and, in their gear, they sat together and consumed the big breakfast that Big Jon prepared for them. Jon gave the team his special tea to drink. Leo looks at the tea, "Big Jon, the last time I drank your special tea I end up ...," suddenly, there was knock at the door interrupting Leo. Sam and Jerry grabbed their guns and when to check it out. As Big Jon sighs with relief thankful for the interruption, Troy looks at his phone as sees that Sean and the rest of the team had arrived as he requested.

Troy gets up and walks to the door. He welcomes his silverback crew into Katrina's home and introduces them to the rest of the team. With the arrival of Troy's ten best men, Leo instructs the team that five of them will stay behind and guard Katrina's home. The rest of the men will secure the delicate package. Carlos yells, "No harm shall come to the package, keep the package alive and well." Troy and Leo question Carlos's concern of the wellbeing of the package. Big Jon taps his cane and tells the brothers to do as Carlos requested. With their new assignment and a full belly, the team was ready for the long night ahead. Mia embraces Anna and kisses her goodbye with great sadness she tells her "Come back to me." Mia, Maria, Katrina, Liz, Sofia, Carlos, and his children left the room and went to the panic room to set up. Carlos touches Junior on the shoulder, "Do you have something for your uncle Leo?" he asks.

Junior sits on the floor and open his bookbag and took out a little black box and gave it to Leo. Leo looks at the box, "Thank you, Junior," he said. Carlos smiles at Leo and tells him, "When it's time to open it, you will know." After a long goodbye the team gets in their trucks and set off to Juan's Farmhouse. The team drove for a few miles before they parked their trucks and walked the rest of the way. Following Carlos's map, they were able to enter the farm from the south side. Leo, Troy, Sam, and Rico get in position to enter the farm to retrieve the special package. While Jerry, Marcus, and Craig cover them from the rear, getting them in and out safely. Anna and Sean will lead the rest of the team and cover the outside of the farmhouse. Sean and his team clear the South side of the farm while Anna moves to the main entrance, clearing that section. Since the team did not have a man on the inside, Leo, Troy, and Rico will have to force their way into the house to get Bella.

On Juan's farm the security was tight as preparations were underway for his cousin, Eli, to visit. Eli only visits the farm once a month to check on his growing grandson. He did not care much about Bella, the child's mother, he just wants his blood line to go on. Eli had promised Juan that he could have Bella as soon as she delivers his grandson. Bella sits alone in her dark room, picking at her nails until they bleed. Her maids came in and gave her a bath. Then they dress her in all black, covering her from head to toe. Once dress the maid brings her to the upper room where she is seated on a lavish couch as she awaits her fate. The maid puts a pillow behind Bella's back, "Your baby will be here any day now, you should be happy," she said. Bella remains quiet. Juan, in in drunken rage barges in and the maid run out of the room fearing that he would strike her for talking to Bella

He rushes over to Bella and pulls her to her feet. He grabs her, pulling her closer to him as he smells her clothing, "I bet you taste as good as you smell," his voice thick with lust as he gropes her as he unbuckles his belt. Nacho walks in, "Eli is here," he announces. Frustrated, Juan pushes him out of his way and goes outside to meet Eli. Nacho looks at Bella and tells her "If I can't have you, no one else can." he rushes out of the room as Bella sit on the couch.

The team looks on from the bushes as they wait for the sun to set. From their location they could see several cars as they pull up to the main house of the farm. Carlos taps into Sam's eyewear for a closer view, "That is Eli, be on standby. I will let you know when to make your move," he alerted Sam. Meanwhile, Carlos, Katrina, and Junior sits on the chairs in the panic room. Everyone sits in silence as they watch the live feed on the monitors. Big Jon observes from a distance as Carlos advises the team to put on their eyewear. So that Junior could create a visual link through their eyewear. The team did as they were told, and Carlos was able to see what the team was seeing.

Troy taps Leo on his shoulder, "You ready?" he asked. Leo looks back at his brother, "Yes, let's get it done." Troy leans back and whispers to Rico, "Stay close and stay behind me." Rico nods with understanding. Anna checks in and lets the team know that they are in position and her area was clear. At the farmhouse, Eli, and his guards were greeted by Juan as he invites them inside. Once they were inside, he presented Eli with three young boys. Eli examined the boys and sent them to his room for the night. These were the gifts that Juan got for his cousin Eli. Eli asked to see his most precious gift and Juan sends two of his guards to fetch Bella. As Nacho stood by his side. She walks into the room timidly and Eli greeted her. He strides over to Bella with an outstretched hand and feels her belly, turning to Juan, "She's passed her due date," he states.

Juan ensures him that his grandson will be here soon and that there was no need to rush. The maid walks over to Eli, "She is a young mother, and it can take time," she said reassuringly. She walks Bella back to her room and locks her in for the night. Bella sits on the bed and stares at the door. With the setting of the sun, the team began to make their way closer to the main house. Leo, Troy, Sam, and Rico move in first and they were able to silently assassinate four of the ground's guards. Marcus and Craig put on their clothing and in disguise they continued to monitor the area. Craig checks in and tells Leo that the entry point is clear. Anna and her team made their way to the lookout tower where Sean and two of his man eliminate the guards, taking over that post. Anna tells Leo that their exit post is clear. With the entrance and the exit of the farmhouse cleared and secured, Leo, Troy, Sam, and Rico begin their advance into the home.

Sam takes the lead and takes out two more guards while Leo

and Troy hide their bodies. Rico stands guard, watching their backs.

Sam follows the map on his watch and leads the team. They cut

through the lounge and headed up the stairs. Sam made it to the top

of the stairs with Leo and Troy trailing behind. Rico was at the foot

of the stairs when suddenly two guards walk in from behind. They

see Rico and Sam seeing the scene from his vantage point quickly

eliminate them. Troy looks at Rico, "Wake up and stay focused," he

says in a steely whisper. Rico nods as Troy helps him to hides the

bodies. Sam cleared the hallway, then they heard talking and

laughter in the next room. Carlos tells the team that Eli and most of

the guards are behind this door. Sam moves on slowly and quietly

followed by Leo, Rico, and Troy.

They made it to Bella's room without any additional

incident. Sam gives his gun to Leo and begins to pick the lock on the

door but struggles to get it open. Rico reaches over and, taking the

two-sided brass plated key, Rico was able to pick the lock in seconds

and open the door. Leo walks inside the room, closing the door

behind him. He sees Bella sitting there on the bed in all black,

covered from head to toe. He checks out the room and the bathroom.

Troy, Rico, and Sam stayed outside, guarding the door. Leo clears the room then he walks up to Bella, "Get up," he barks, but she did

not move. He pulls her to her feet "Walk…," he commanded, and

again, she did not move. He pushes her to move, and she lifts her

dress. Leo looks down and sees that her feet were chained to the bed.

Carlos taps into Leo's eyewear and tells him how to remove

the locks. Leo cuts the locks and Bella shows him the chains on her

wrist. He cuts the chains, freeing them from her wrist. Leo grabs her

arm and begins to push her towards the door. As he started to walk,

she yanks her arm away from Leo. Impatient, he pulls his gun on her.

She slightly lifts her black face covering only exposing her mouth.

As she slowly opens her mouth Leo peers inside her mouth and sees

a red flashing tracking device implanted in her tooth.

He pushes Bella over to the bed. Heavily pregnant Bella lays

down on her back and opens her mouth. Carlos tells Leo to pull out

the tracker without breaking it. Leo goes to the door and asks Sam

for the pliers. Sam looks confused as he hands Leo the tool while

Troy and Rico continue to keep watch. Bella braces herself and she

did not cry, Leo wonders is she was unable to speak. He walks back

over to Bella and places the pliers in her mouth, carefully pulling out

her tooth affixed with the tracking device. Bella sits up and spits out

the blood from her mouth. Then she stood up and shows Leo the shock collar around her neck. Leo asked Carlos how to remover the collar Carlos tells him step by step how to remove the device without setting off the alarm. Leo was able to safely remove the collar then he spotted the birthmark on her neck in the shape of the moon.

Chapter Sixteen

Leo rubs his finger on Bella's birthmark. He looks at her as she slowly removes her black face covering. Leo looks down at her face, as he gently lifts her chin, she looks up at him. Leo's heart stops as he looks in Leanna's dark brown eyes. Carlos gasps for air as he screams for Big Jon. Big Jon comes running over to the monitor and immediately collapses into the chair, clutching his chest. Carlos notifies the team, "The package is secure, the package is secure, the package is Leanna!"

Marcus and Craig look at each other, "What about the package...?" Sam, Troy, and Rico open the door and look on as if they had seen a ghost. Carlos excitedly repeats himself, "The package is Leanna, she is alive! Anna taps in on the feed, "We got two cars coming to the north entrance, time for you guys to move." Sean started to make his way over to that area, Anna told her team to stay her as she joins Sean. Leo embraces Leanna. She stood still, lost in time unable to determine if she was in a dream. She did not speak as the tear fell from her eye as Leo leads her to the door, he tells Sam "Move out."

Suddenly, Juan opens the door across from Leanna's room. Leo pushes Leanna back into her room and Sam, Troy, and Rico followed, hiding in the bathroom. Leo quickly covers Leanna's face and sits her on the bed. Standing outside of Bella room Juan sends Nacho to tell the servants to set the table for dinner. Nacho did not what to leave Juan and lone with Bella, but he did as he was told. He hurries down the stairs and went to the dining room. Juan walks in the room and told Leanna, "The doctor is here now. Tonight, you will have the baby." Quietly, Leo reaches out from behind the door and grabs Juan, covering his mouth. Expeditiously, he slits Juan's throat, holding him as he bleeds to the ground.

He signals Troy and Rico to assassinate everyone in the other room. Leo helps Leanna up on her feet and walks her over to the door while Sam walks ahead of them. Troy and Rico assassinate the people in the other room, but Eli was not among them. He had stepped out just as Juan walked into Leanna's room. At the gate Anna and Sean greets the drivers as they show them were to park. Sean keeps a close watch as Anna searches the vehicle and sees that it was the doctor and his staff. She asks, "what are you doing here?"

The doctor sighs, "Bella is going to have her baby." Anna opens the car door and tells Sean to escort them to Bella's room. She radios in to let the team know that Sean is escorting the doctor and his staff to Bella's room.

Copying the alert, Leo signals to his team to get on the move. "Move out, and protect Leanna," he ordered. Before they could get to the stairs, Leanna panics and runs to the dark hallway. Leo gives chase and manages to grab her, pushing her against the wall. He holds her and calls her name, "Leanna! Leanna—, baby please look at me. Please see me... I'm here baby... I'm here." He kisses her face as he held her in his arms. Leanna tries to speak but she was weak, and her voice was raspy, "Leo— your dead." Sam comes over to Leo, "We have to move." Troy and Rico quickly follow. They stood in the dark hallway in silence as they could hear the doctor and his staff coming up the stairs.

The doctors enter the room with his staff he looks around the room and asks, "Where is Bella?" "She must be in the restroom," Sean responds to the doctor as the last member of the medical staff enter the room, Sean shoots them in the brow. Troy slowly walks back to Bells room and saw that it was Sean he signals for him to fall in line as they head back to the exits.

On the way down the stairs Rico hears a child crying, he stops. Leo tells him to keep moving. Remembering what Carlos told him he opens the door. There he sees one of Eli guards beating a young child. Seeing Rico, the guard screams for help. Rico empties all his rounds into the guard's chest. The rest of Eli's guards came running to see what was going on. The boys ran out of the room and down the stairs when the guards open fire, killing all three of the boys.

Anna hears the gun fire and decides to send in Marcus and Craig to help Leo. She radios in, telling the team at the south entrance to get ready. As Marcus and Craig move slowly, entering through the front doors, Eli's guards walk forward to greet them, falling for their ruse, because the duo were dressed as Juan's guards. Marcus and Craig play the part. As they get closer to Eli's guards, the team eliminates them. They hear footsteps coming down the stairs. Craig and Marcus look up and see that Bella was Leanna. Without any hesitation they join in and surrounded her, protecting her with their lives as they fought their way out of the farmhouse. Craig and Marcus throw their home-made bombs into the home as the team make their way over to Anna. The flames sent the workers and their children running into the valley as they desperately try to escape from the farm. Nacho came from the shadows and saw the fire as the workers run to the deep valley. He looks over and saw that Bella was being taken by armed men. He hides in the dark as he watches the exchange.

Carlos taps in on the radio, "Anna the package is coming your way." Anna and Jerry wait anxiously for the team to arrive. As she peers into the flames, Anna sees Troy, Craig, Sam, Marcus, Sean, and Leo making their way toward the waiting group from a distance, but she could not see who they were protecting. Suddenly, Eli and four of his personal guard's spring from the side of the house in an ambush cutting off Anna and Jerry from the rest of the team. The farmhouse was on fire. Leo and the people he cared about stood trapped between the burning building and Eli and his vengeful guards. "Release her!" Eli commanded. The team kept their guns pointed at Eli and his guards.

Eli keeps his gaze fixed, "Bella come to me," he ordered again. She did not move. He yells for her to come to him again, she jumps. Leo and the team move in closer using their bodies as shield to protect her. He yells "what do you want with this woman, she belongs to me." Leo yells "why does she belongs to you?" Frustrated as he ignored the question Eli offers Leo's team money if they would bring him Bella. When the team did not accept his request, he became blind with fury, and he orders his guards to kill Bella and to cut out the baby from her belly. Bella takes a few steps forward and removes her head covering, exposing her entire face and hair. She looks over at Anna.

"Leanna—" Anna mouthed, seeing that Bella was in fact Leanna, she glances at Leo. In that moment Anna had flash backs. Her head full of memories of her and Leanna as kids playing in the yard. The day she left home and then the images of her dead sister. Anna stumbles as she looks at Jerry in disbelief, she opens fire on Eli's guards as Jerry join in. Leo, Sam, Troy, and Sean cover Leanna protecting her from the gun fire. Craig and Marcus join in and open fire executing Eli's guards.

As the hail of bullets ceased, Eli was the only one standing as all his guards fell to the ground. Overcome with emotion. Anna runs over to embrace Leanna when suddenly Eli gets up and pulls out his gun as he takes aim at Anna. Before he could squeeze off his trigger, Leo walks over the Eli shooting him in the hand. Eli drops his gun as he screams in agony, Leo rapidly squeezing the trigger even though he was out of bullets. He walks up to Eli and grabs his throat "she is carrying my child" he yells as he rips Eli tongue out of his mouth. Eli fell to the ground as he choaking on his own blood. Upon seeing the Nacho disarmed himself and runs off the valley with the rest of the workers.

Anna embraces Leanna, as the team made their way down the valley to the south entrance. Leo held Leanna close to him protecting her and covering her eyes from the bodies lying on the grass. There they meet up with the rest of the silverback's team making their way to their cars. Troy saw that Rico was missing, and once again Leo was faced with leaving Leanna. Leanna kisses Leo, with her weak raspy voice she tells him "Go get him, and come back to us," she said as she held her heavily pregnant belly. Leo tells Sam, Marcus, Craig, Anna, and Jerry to get Leanna back to the barn safely and to protect her at all costs as he walks off. Troy tells the rest of his silverback's team to see this through. Troy, and Sean followed Leo as he makes his way in the dark back to the burning farm to get Rico.

Chapter Seventeen

Anna leads the team as they return to their vehicles and heads back to the barn. Leo and his team went back to the farm to find Rico. They hear someone over in the bushes and Troy signals the team to circle around and check it out. Leo, with his AK47 drawn walks forward slowly in the darkness of the night. Sean went to the left while Troy went to the right and the team moves in with their guns drawn. They slowly approached the bushes and found several women and their children hiding.

Sean told them to leave the area and head down the valley to the main road. The women and their children left in a hurry, thanking them. The team continue to search the farm for Rico when they came across an old man who was trying to help some of the burned victims. The old man begs the team not hurt them. Leo asks the old man if there was anyone else alive on the farm. The old man slowly raises his head, "Yes, they are hiding," he says. Troy tells the old man to take them to the people who are hiding and assigns Sean to stay and keep watch of the area.

The old man led Leo and Troy to the other people that were hiding on the farm. Leo and Troy try to help the injured people as they got up and walk back to Sean. The old man saw that they were good men and that their intensions were good. The old man tells Troy, "Juan has many people on this farm that he has stolen, sold, and enslaved. The people will help you, but they are scared." The old man went on to tell the team that he was taken from his home over forty years ago, when Juan's father took his wife for his own. His wife later took her own life due to the abuse she was subjected too on the farm. He continues to tell them that he was forced to eat his wife's flesh as Juan's father made Juan and his guards watched.

The old man points at an old hut in the distance, "That is where it happened." Tears welled in the old man eyes as he tells Leo, "Juan's cousin Eli used to come visit with his two sons Mark and Luke. They would use the women and children to practice on as their dad teaches them how to carve. The people that they killed was then feed to the workers and sold as meat." The old man sits and rest for a while after recounting the disturbing story. Troy tells Sean to stay and help the people to get to safety.

With their guns drawn Leo and Troy move on slowly, continuing their search for Rico in the darkness of the night. They hear a woman calling for help as she runs over to them, falling to her feet begging for them to help her. She told Leo and Troy that her daughter was trapped in the basement and a man went in to help, but the man and her daughter has not returned. Troy asks what the man looks like, and she points at Leo. That man could only be Rico. Leo and Troy radio to tell the rest of the team their location. Carlos calls Sean and tells him to follow Leo and Troy and clear the area because Juan still has men out there.

Troy opens his water bottle and pours the contents onto some towels, handing one to Leo. They wrap the towels around their faces and made their way over to the entrance of the burnt building and down to the basement. Anna hears Carlos telling Sean that more of Juan's guards could be in the area. She pulls the car over and tells Jerry and Craig that they should go help Leo. Jerry and Craig look over at Sam for his approval. Sam looks at them for a moment, "Take the truck and go, I will protect Leanna." Jerry and Craig made a U-turn and headed back to Juan's farm. Anna and the rest of her team pulls off and they head for Katrina's farm. Carlos sees them on the cameras he tells Maria and Katrina to meet the team and escorted them to the barn and into the panic room safely. Carlos radios into

Leo and tells him that Leanna and rest of the team made it back and are safe and secure.

With this good news Leo felt at ease, Troy pulls out his flashlights and enter the basement as Leo closely follows him. They call out to see if there was anyone in the basement. They could hear footsteps coming closer towards them from the darkness. With their guns drawn, they wait to see who will emerge from the dark basement. In a distance Troy see Rico carrying a little girl followed by two women and three children. Rico smiled, "Took you long enough," he said handing over the little girl to Troy as they help the people to safety. Once out of the basement, Sean met up with the team. As the people wait for them to return, the old man assures the scared people that the men are there to help them.

The team approaches the old man as he looks on, they sit and rest for a while. Not noticing that there were several of Juan's guards that tried to blend in with the people. Sean handed one of the injured children to a man. The child screams and would not let go of Sean. This draws the attention of the team and Troy asks the child, "Why are you scared?" The child whimpered, "He is one of the bad men." Leo pulls his gun and raises it to the man's head. The man begs for his life and tells the team that he was a guard and that he was not going to hurt them. Rico did not want to hear what the man had to say. He pulls out his gun and assassinates the man in front of his team and the injured people.

This sends the rest of the guards running into the night. Sean, Leo, and Troy went after them. Troy looks back and yells at Rico to stay with the people. He was not happy with the order but knowing that his brothers were upset Rico did as he was told. Leo, Troy, and Sean took off in the opposite direction hunting down the men in the dark. Thirty minutes later as the people sit in the dark with a small campfire they went to sleep. Rico heard a noise in the distance. Positioning himself to defend the people, he keeps his eyes trained in the direction of the noise when he sees, over in the mist, Craig, and Jerry.

He signals to them, and the two men join him by the fire while Rico fills them in. Throughout the night Leo, Troy, and Sean searches for the rest of the guards finding and eliminating three of the guards. Leo desperately wanted to get back to Leanna. Making no progress in locating the rest of the guards. He calls off the search and they head back to Rico and the people. As they enter the camp site, they smile at the sight of Craig and Jerry. Leo asked them if Leanna was okay, they both reply that she was with Sam. As the workers pack up, they had no were to go. Leo told the people that they were free to go but to be careful because some of the guards are still in the woods. Some of the people left in a hurry while the others stayed in fear that they might be caught by the guards. The team talks among themselves trying to decide what to do with the scared people. Leo told the team to gather the people as they started to make their way back to Katrina's farm.

At Katrina's farm Maria cares for Leanna while Anna and the rest of the women look on. Sofia made a hardy bowl of soup and Anna fed Leanna. Leanna asked Katrina if she could have a bath and she clucks her tongue saying, "This is your home, and you don't have to ask to do anything." Maria helps Leanna up while Mia fills the tub with water. Maria walks Leanna to the bathroom and helps her to undress. Maria and Mia could see the scars on Leanna's belly where Luke carved his name into her skin. The women look at each other as they help Leanna to get into the tub. Maria tells Anna to go find Leanna some clean clothing. Maria stays with Leanna, holding back her tears as she washes Leanna's bruised, thin, fragile body.

On the cameras Carlos, Junior, and Big Jon see the team coming up to the farm with a lot of people following behind them. Big Jon urgently pops into the room and tells Katrina. They both rushed outside to meet the team and the people. Katrina calls for Sofia and Mia to bring food and water to the back of the farm for the survivors of Juan's evil operation. Leo greets Katrina and Big Jon and fills them in on what happened at Juan's farm. Katrina tells Big Jon to tell the survivors that they can go to the back of the farm. Leo tells Sam, Craig, Jerry, and Marcus to go help the people and keep their eyes open for Juan's other guards. Troy tells his men to cover the area and that no one is allowed to enter or leave the farm. With Katrina's farm on tight security, Leo rushes into the house to see Leanna.

Leo enters Leanna's room slowly opening the door. He could see Maria washing her in the bathroom. Leanna gets out of the bathtub and Leo could see her through the open door. He looks at her thin fragile body he sees the scars on her neck, back, thighs, arms, and belly. Leanna looks in the mirror at her reflection and sees the scars on her belly. She reaches for the washcloth and begins to scrub her belly roughly. Maria goes over to Leanna and covers her up with a robe and comforts her. Leo tries to control his temper; he steps back colliding with the bookshelf with a dull thud. Leanna hears the sound, looking over she sees Leo.

Chapter Eighteen

Leo sits on the bed with his head down. Maria walks Leanna over to him and left the room. Leanna moves closer to Leo, and he sees her belly, kissing her growing mound as he weeps. Leanna embraces him as she sits by him and in a weak and raspy voice she tells him, "I never stopped loving you. Our son will be here soon." Leo looks over at her and sees the marks on her neck. He leans over to kiss her, but she pulls back, turning her face away from his view. This throws Leo off, and he gets up, quickly leaving the room and bumping into Maria. He went outside to the back of the farm. Maria rushes into the room to see if Leanna was okay.

Leanna stood up and Maria dressed her then Leanna gets back in the bed and went to sleep. Maria closes the door and goes to find Leo. He was getting his team together to go hunt for the rest of Juan's guards. Maria told Carlos to stop this madness. Carlos and Big Jon try to stop Leo, but he would not listen to them. Troy walks in on the confrontation and Maria begs Troy to tell Leo not to go. As the survivors looks on at the spectacle that was taking place before them, the women held their children close to them. Troy notices this and told his men that no one is allowed to leave or enter the farm. Rico agrees with Troy's order. He tells Leo, "We should rest tonight and think it over, let them come to us."

"They will pay for what they did to Leanna!" Leo yells. Anna agrees with Leo, "No, we need to hunt them tonight," she said defiantly. Now Troy's team and Leo's team stood face to face and ready to fight each other. Big Jon taps his cane, "Enough—, enough I say! No one is leaving this farm tonight." He tells Sam to take Leo and walk it off. Big Jon told the silverback's team to guard the farm and Leo's team to stand down. Big Jon then turns to Katrina, Mia, and Sofia and tell them to go prepare dinner for everyone. The old man heard Big Jon and he instructs some of the women in the group to help them. Katrina, Mia, and Sofia did as they were told while Leo's team stood down. Anna went to check on Leo and Sam. She walked into the house just as Leo and Sam were planning the leave on their own. She called to Sam and told him that Big Jon needed his help outside. With Sam gone, Anna was able to calm Leo down. She pulls out a chair and sits down, "Leo, let's get some rest tonight and make our move tomorrow. Leanna is here now, and she needs you." She gets up and walks over to Leo, "I saw her in the bath, she went through hell. She would not want you to go out there like this. Your son could be here any day now, so don't do anything stupid." They stood there in silence, then Anna whispered to Leo "I have something important to tell you, but not here". She looks at Leo with regret, Leo crosses his arm as he looks on in confusion.

Troy and Rico enter the room and Anna leaves to go check on Mia in the kitchen. Troy and Rico were able to talk Leo out of going back to Juan's farm. The brothers talk for a few and share in some laughter. That night the two teams put their difference aside and eat dinner outside by the campfire. After a long forty-eight hours, Leo went to his room and took a long hot bath. He could not stop thinking about the possibility of Juan's men coming back for Leanna. Maria knocks on his room door. Hearing a knock, Leo he rushes out the bath and opens the door.

Maria tells Leo that Leanna is awake, and she is asking for him. He gets dressed and quickly arrives at Leanna's room. She was still lying-in bed but sat up once Leo entered and asked him to sit by her. She takes his hand and puts it on her belly. For the first time, Leo could feel his son moving. He smiles at her, "Is that him moving?" he asks excitedly.

Leanna laughs, "Yes," she answered smiling. Then suddenly she begins to cry. Leo embraces her and she kisses him. That night Leanna and Leo laid in bed, and she tells him everything that happened to her. She blames herself for everything that happened, and Leo ensures her that it was not her fault. Leanna tells Leo that she wants to go home. That night Leo held Leanna in his arms and did not let her go.

In the morning Leo askes to meet with his brothers in private. He tells his brothers that he is going to take Leanna home. Troy and Rico agree that he should take his team and get her home safely. Troy told Leo that he will keep hunting for Juan's guards, and he won't stop until they were all dead. Rico asks Troy if he could help. As Troy, Rico and the rest of the silverback's team pack up to go, A few of the men that worked on Juan's farm asked to join them in the search. Troy told Sean to stay at Katrina's farm as her personal guard and to help get the farm up and running.

Leo met with the rest of his team and told them that he was taking Leanna home while Troy and Rico hunt for the rest of Juan's guards. Leo thanks Katrina for everything. She kisses Leo on the lips and told him to let her know when the baby arrives. She walks off holding Sean's hand. Sean told Leo that he will keep in touch. Big

Jon decides to stay on the farm and help Katrina for a while. He taps his cane, "There is a lot of work that needs to be done. Now that we have the help, we must get this farm up and running. Katrina can start her farming again if that is okay with you." Leo ensures Big Jon that Katrina can stay on the farm if she wants, and that the farm will always be her home.

Sam, Marcus, Craig, and Jerry look over at Leo. As he walks over to them, Jerry yells "You're not getting rid of us so easy…. we are coming with you!" They laugh together as Sam raises his hands above his head, "Get ready— we're going home boys!" he exclaimed, the friends joining in with a hail of excitement. As the team packs their vans for the long trip, Carlos went to visit Leanna in her room. Leanna thanks him for everything he has done for her. She apologizes to Carlos for not believing him when he told her that he was a friend of Leo and for refusing his help.

Carlos began to warn her, "You're going home, and Leo should not know…." Just then, Leo walks into the room and interrupted their conversation. Leanna gets up and Leo lovingly walks over to help her. After a long goodbye Carlos pulls Leo to the side and tells him that he will be tracking all the teams. Leo thanks Carlos for everything. Junior runs up to his uncle and gave him a matching bracelet for his son. Leo picks Junior up and hugs him. Maria walks over with her daughter and Leo hugs and kisses them good-bye. Anna and Mia were all packed as they helped Leanna to the van, with Leo running over to assist. Sam tells Carlos, "We got it from here. Get some rest and enjoy your family." Carlos told Sam that Katrina asked them to stay on the farm with her. Jerry, Marcus, and Craig tell him that he should.

Leo starts the van, and they get ready for the long drive ahead of them. Craig, Sam, Jerry, and Marcus followed behind them in a truck. It was nighttime when they pulled up to Leanna's home. Leo jumped out of the van and told his team to go home and get some rest. They refused to leave and went to check out the back of the house. The lights were on, but Leanna did not recognize her home. Leo ensures her that this was their home. Anna and Mia walked in, and Leo helps Leanna out the van as they slowly walk into the house.

There Leanna sees her friends Laura, Michelle, Tracy, Sara, and her mother. Her friends rush over to embrace her as they kiss her bruised face and touches her belly. Leanna's mom slowly walks over and hugs Leanna as she cries. Anna walks over and hugs them both.

Leo and Mia unpack the van and then they settle down and have dinner.

Leanna could see that her friends really missed her as they made plans for the next day. It was time for them to go home as her friends left for the night, so did Leo's team. Anna told Leo that she was going to take her mom home and spend the night there. Mia askes to go with her and soon they all depart. With the couple now alone, Leanna walks around her room, looking at how different everything was in her home. Leo walks in and sees her face, he sits on the bed, "Before I left, I told your friends to do a makeover. I was going to sell it." She looks at him, "Going to….?" she questioned. Leo gets up and walks over to her, "This is our home, and our son will need a home." Leanna walks off and went to the bathroom.

Leo opens the closet and gets a blanket and a pillow off the bed. He leaves the room and closes the door behind him. He walks over to the couch and puts his pillow and blanket on the couch, lays down and closes his eyes for a few seconds. He smiles as he remembers that morning when Leanna was jumping on the couch as he watched her from the window. He asks himself "is the Leanna I knew, and love gone forever?" He sits up on the couch and with his head down, he thinks about how different things were going to be from now on. He takes out his phone and calls Carlos to check on his brothers. Carlos assures him that his brothers are okay and are still looking for the rest of Juan's guards.

Leo gets off the phone and reaches in his jacket and found the box that Junior gave him. He opens the box and looks at the gift, he reaches for the phone and call Carlos and thank him for the gift, then he heard Leanna he quickly ends the call.

Chapter Nineteen

Leanna opens the bathroom door and did not see Leo. She walks over and opens her room door then she sits on the bed. Leo saw that the door was open, he enters the room and sees her sitting there. He sits down next to her, "Are you okay?" he asks. Leanna looks up at him holding back her tears, "Yes, I'm home…!" she says as realization set in. She lays on the bed and Leo lays by her side, holding her in his arms, he smells her hair. Leanna smiles "I missed this." She looks up at Leo and kisses him. Leo kisses Leanna back as he wishes they could kiss forever.

Leanna gets up and undresses herself as Leo watches her. Leo sits up on the bed and looks at her as she crawls back on the bed, he embraces her. He gently kisses her scars, and her belly as he tells her that his love for her has not change. Leo held her as he embraces her, not wanting the moment to end as he felt alive as he kisses her. That night Leo made love to Leanna as they were both filled with emotions of pleasure and pain. In the morning Leo's phone rings and it was Carlos checking in and to inform Leo that Troy and Rico were still on the hunt. He reported that everyone was doing good and for Leo not to worry. Leo told him to check in every three days, Carlos agrees as he ended the call. Leo got up and went to the bathroom. He gets dressed and looks over at Leanna just like he did the first night they made love. He falls in love with her all over again. He took out the gift that Carlos gave him and puts it by Leanna as she slept. Then he went to the kitchen and made her breakfast.

Leanna wakes up and saw the gift that Leo left behind. She opens it and smiles. She rushes to the bathroom to freshen up and quickly gets dressed. She slowly walks into the kitchen and sees Leo outside by the pool. She opens the sliding door and walks outside, as Leo pulls out the chair for her. She gently sits and have breakfast with Leo. Leanna gave Leo the box as she sat in silence. Leo smiled and got down on one knee, "Leanna will you marry me" he asked as he put the ring on her finger and kisses her hand.

Leo could see her belly moving as his son moves and kicks. He kisses her belly and Leanna told him that she was eight months pregnant. She looks over to the fence, "Luke told me that he was watching us for months. That night when he raped me his dad called, and Luke told him that he had a gift for him. I was the gift. Later that week his dad came for me, but Luke never showed up, and I was sent to Juan's farm," she recounted somberly.

Leo was upset that Leanna had to go through this he gets up, "I don't' want to hear anymore." Leanna tells him to sit down and listen, she takes a sip of her orange juice. Leo sits down and looks over at Leanna, she holds his hand, "You need to hear this." She went on the tell Leo that she lied to Eli and told him that she was carrying Luke's child. With the loss of Mark and Luke, this child was all Eli had. This was the only way Leanna would survive Juan's farm. Once Eli found out she was carrying Luke's child, he ordered his guards to protect her. Leanna looks Leo in the eyes, "When Eli kidnaped Carlos, he told the guards that Luke was dead, and I knew that you were the one that killed him. I heard Carlos, as he told the stories of how Luke begged when he came face to face with the lion. Carlos told me that he was a friend of yours, and that you would come looking for him." She begins to cry as she tells Leo that Carlos tried to help her to escape. He was caught because of the tracker in her mouth. Carlos was then beaten and forced to kill a man and eat his flesh. While Juan, Eli and their guards laugh and threw broken beer bottles at him.

Leanna looks over at Leo with tears in her eyes, Leo comforts her and as he tells her that this is all over now and no one will ever harm her again. Leanna smiles at him and then the doorbell rings. Leo brings Leanna inside and she sits on the couch as he went to see who had arrived. He opened the door he sees a lady looking at the house. Leo asks her "can I help you?" The lady asked if the house was still for sale Leo told her no. Leanna smiles at hearing the exchange. The lady apologizes for the mistake and walks off as Leo closes the door and returns to sit and talk with Leanna some more. The lady stood outside as she stares at the house, she puts her sunglasses on "what a pity" then she walks off. Later that night Leanna and Leo were getting ready for bed when Leanna passed out and fell in the kitchen. Leo rushes over to pick her up and saw water on the floor. Leo did not know what to do so he calls Sam, who advises Leo to take her to the hospital.

Sam calls the team and tells them that Leanna was hurt. Laura, Sara, Michelle, and Tracy met them at the hospital. Jerry, Craig, Sam, and Marcus pulled up a few minutes later. Leo lifts Leanna in his arm and takes her inside the hospital yelling for help. He remembers the last time he was there. He goes up to the desk and the nurses brings Leanna to the same room, number seven. They push Leo out of the room, as Sara sneaks into the room to be with Leanna. The nurse calls code BLUE. Leo looks on, standing there in shock as the nurses and doctors run past him, pushing a baby incubator and medical instruments. Sam and the rest of the team comfort Leo as he fell to the floor. Anna, Mia, and Leanna's mom came running up to Leo as Sam tries to calm them down.

That night the sky turns black as the clouds cover the moon and rain begins to fall. The loud sound of the thunder shakes the hospital. Leo felt the cold air as his blood runs cold. He gets up and slowly walks outside into the rain and fell to his knees, giving up on life. His team gathers around him. He looks up at the night sky as the rain falls on his face he whispered, "let me live again...." The sound of the thunder sets off several car alarms as Leo surrender to his fate.

Sara runs out yelling, "Leo —your son is here!" Leo hurries to his feet and quickly returns to the hospital. Running through the door, tripping over the cart that was in the hallway. He rushes to Leanna's room and see's Leanna holding their son. Leanna smiles at Leo and in her weak raspy voice says, "Come and meet your son." The nurses stop Leo and dries off his face. Leo walks over and stoops down, he kisses Leanna and looks at his son, "Eric," he said proudly.

Eric was finally here, and even though this was not the way Leanna and Leo wanted him to enter the world. This was the way Eric "The Forever Ruler" made his entrance into the world. Leo held his son in his arms and kissed him. Leo looks over at Sam and saw that look in Leo's eyes. The look of the Lion who will do anything to protect his pride. Everyone came running to the room to see Eric. Carlos even hacked into the hospital cameras as they celebrate the birth of Eric. Leanna looks over at Leo and she sees the man she fell in love with. She decides to no longer speak of the pass. She decided that they would move on from this to keep her family safe.

She looks at her engagement ring, pressing and holding the diamond on the ring. Junior's game beeps, he looks at his computer screen "Auntie Leanna, I can see you! Welcome to the game." Junior rushes over and shows his dad his game. Carlos smiles and askes Junior if he was ready for his own adventure. Junior smiled at his dad as his dad continued to monitor Troy and Sean's location.